The Backyard Traveler Returns

62 Outings in Southern, Eastern and Historic Nevada

by

RICHARD MORENO

Published by
The Carson City Children's Museum

1 9 9 2

Other Books By Richard Moreno:

The Backyard Traveler, 54 Outings in Northern Nevada (1991)

THE BACKYARD TRAVELER RETURNS
62 Outings in Southern, Eastern and Historic Nevada
Copyright 1992 by Richard Moreno

Published by the Carson City Children's Museum

ISBN 0-9631205-1-4

Cover art by J. Ross Browne

Photographs by Richard Moreno unless otherwise noted.

Dedicated once again to Hank, the littlest
"Backyard Traveler."

Contents

CONTENTS

CONTENTS

Preface

Thanks once again to Rich Moreno for his generous support of the Children's Museum project here in Carson City.

Proceeds generated by his first book helped enable the museum to move toward its goal of raising enough money so that it can create a special place for children to learn, explore and, at the same time, have fun.

And we expect readers will enjoy the opportunity to rejoin him, in this companion volume, by exploring the many backroads and fascinating places found throughout Nevada.

As the museum progresses toward the day it opens its doors, gifts like Mr. Moreno's become critical for the timely completion of a first class youth and family museum in Nevada's capital city. Visitors can anticipate displays and exhibits allowing them to explore the arts, science and the humanities, all within the confines of a handsomely restored building.

Renovation construction is underway, exhibits are on the drawing board and the museum's supporters are ready to provide a quality educational experience for the kid in each of us!

So we invite you to buy a book (or more — give them as gifts!) and show your support for this vital project.

THE CARSON CITY
CHILDREN'S MUSEUM
BOARD OF DIRECTORS:

Linda Ponn, *President*
Joan Zadny, *Secretary*
Sandy Hatchell, *Treasurer*
Suzi Meehan, *Fundraising Chair*
Anne Macquarie, *Executive Director*
Deana Guthrie
Jenny Kilpatrick
Leeandra Shaw

Foreword

THE BEST "NEW BOOK" NEWS I've come across in more than a year is that Richard Moreno, the Backyard Traveler, is giving us this reprise. The last time I felt this good was when he came to us with that first Backyard Traveler.

"The Backyard Traveler Returns" is simply a dandy treat for those who love Nevada already. To you who have yet to savor the Silver State's joyous rural places, Rich's new book is pure helpmate.

I am particularly pleased that he includes here so many fine pieces on the great southern part of our state. The reader is going to find a virtual Moreno Road Map to some of the most exciting scenes in America. And we're not talking about the more heralded neon. Rich Moreno is dwelling herein on museums, on the wonder of Hoover Dam, and he gets us off smartly with a concise profile of "Historic Las Vegas."

His longtime practice of not only getting out into the "real" Nevada, but of meticulously setting down what he sees and feels and enjoys out there, profits readers. When Rich Moreno writes of Boulder City — Nevada's Garden City — you are seized with the notion that maybe its high time you saw it for yourself — or revisited, assuming you're already acquainted with this charming Nevada community.

This is a representative statewide glimpse of Nevada, too. Rich Moreno gives us some important insight into the state's fading heritage — its ghost towns. While he's at it, he reaffirms the importance of each of us respecting the fragile nature of these places. Vandals already have taken a heavy toll, and this author declares emphatically that each of us has a responsibility to put a stop to tearing down what remains of our past.

The ghost town chapter is among the chief strengths of this charming book. Rich transports us to "Nevada's best surviving ghost place — Belmont." Thanks to him, we see Candelaria, and Hamilton, and the faded glory of Manhattan out in Nye County; the place with the glorious name — Metropolis — and through his words, we see Kingston Canyon, and Rhyolite.

This is a book with the credibility that is Rich Moreno's hallmark. He is mighty careful in his faithful research. His writing again is bright, interesting, helpful.

Thanks to him and to the many who joined in the effort to reward readers' once again. Their sterling contributions deserve our warmest applause.

ROLLAN MELTON
Reno Gazette-Journal

Introduction

THE BACKYARD TRAVELER RETURNS
62 Outings in southern, eastern and historic Nevada

THOSE OF YOU who were with me for the earlier volume of this series ("The Backyard Traveler: 54 Outings in Northern Nevada" — available at bookstores everywhere) may recall I threatened to do another dealing with the rest of the state if that one was well received.

It did well — thank God, because I would have felt so bad about saddling the Carson City Children's Museum with a loser, I would have had to buy up all the leftover copies so they wouldn't lose money — and the result is "The Backyard Traveler Returns."

As with the first volume, the day trips and outings featured in this book are drawn from my weekly columns that have appeared for more than five years in "The Nevada Appeal" newspaper in Carson City (as well as in a few other places). As I mentioned in the earlier book, it is not my intention to write the last word on any of the places or subjects found here. Rather, my columns and this book are my attempts to provide the casual traveler/reader with a little background, some history and a bit of the flavor and feel for interesting places found throughout Nevada.

More than two years ago, when I first sat down to compile an outline for some kind of "Backyard Traveler" book, I wrote a list of all the columns I wanted to include. Not surprisingly, the list was extremely long and the book would have been unwieldy. Out of necessity, I had to chop that outline into two pieces and tackle only those places more or less north of Goldfield. Even then, I wasn't entirely true to my goal, as the ghost town of Goldpoint, located 35 miles south of Goldfield, somehow snuck into that first book.

That meant, of course, leaving many places out. This second book provides me with an opportunity to rectify the situation and share my observations about a second group of equally fascinating historic sites, friendly small towns and beautiful scenic areas. Additionally, it gives me a chance to write about some aspects of the state's largest city, Las Vegas, that don't get much attention, such as its museums, historic places and natural attractions.

"The Backyard Traveler Returns" also features some of the less well-known communities and sites along Highway 95 (the west side of the state) and Highway 93 (the east side). These two ribbons of road pass through some pretty nice country that, if you drive a little way off the main roads, offer more than meets the eye. For instance, the greatest concentration of state parks in Nevada is in Lincoln County, just off Highway 93, while there are some excellent ghost towns, like Rhyolite and Candelaria, just off Highway 95.

Because ghost town hunting is one of my passions, I've included a special chapter on the historical Nevada, spotlighting nearly a dozen of the more accessible and/or interesting ghost towns in various parts of the state. One point I can't stress enough — and those who read the first book recall my essay on ghost towns — is the importance of respecting ghost towns and historic sites. Do not take anything you find in a ghost town. Do not use a metal detector to dig up historic sites or ghost towns. Please look, take pictures if you want and leave it there for someone else to enjoy later. Weather and time do enough damage to these places without people accelerating the destruction and decay.

The last chapter in this book is a potpourri of places that perhaps could have been included in the earlier book — except for the fact they hadn't yet been written when I put that book together. These columns are just a handful of special places that were interesting to me. They range from the evocative post-holocaust ruins of American Flats to the semi-provocative Basque carvings in a picturesque meadow above Glenbrook. I've also included the fine Stewart Indian Museum in Carson City and the historic Tallac Historic Site on the southwestern shore of Lake Tahoe.

There are a number of people responsible for this book. Foremost are the folks at the Carson City Children's Museum, who, once again, have agreed to serve as my publishers. They are very special people who have a wonderful dream — turning the former Civic Auditorium in Carson City into a hands-on museum for children — that I want to see become a reality as soon as possible.

Thanks, in particular, go to Suzi Meehan, my liaison with the museum, who edited both volumes and provided moral support throughout the process of writing, assembling and rewriting. Additionally, I again thank Nevada Appeal Editor Don Ham, who started all of this in 1987 by inviting me to write a weekly travel column. I'm also indebted to Sandi Wright, who edits my weekly columns, Appeal photographer Eugene Jack, who transforms my negatives into something usable, and to former Appeal photographer Lisa Tolda, who, for so many years, offered kind words of encouragement. Special thanks also to the Appeal's Dale Wetenkamp, Rich Johnston of the Nevada Department of Transportation, the Las Vegas News Bureau and all the other folks who lent me photos for this book.

Of course, the greatest source of inspiration for this book is my beautiful son Hank, who has hiked on the Pacific Crest Trail, wandered the historic grounds at Tallac, retraced the Pony Express route and patiently ridden with me on those long, dusty roads leading off to a half-dozen ghost towns.

RICHARD MORENO
September, 1992

PART I

The
Neon
Desert

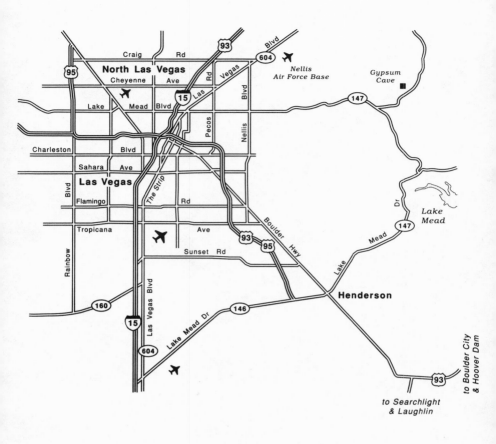

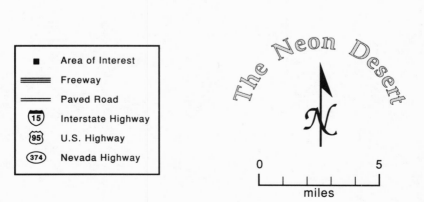

The Neon Desert

GOING TO LAS VEGAS is one of those secret pleasures we all hate to acknowledge. It's outrageous, scandalous and bizarre, wonderful, magical and incredible. In a world of bland, 'it's-the-right-thing-to-do' oatmeal, Las Vegas is sweet hot fudge sundaes and cotton candy.

Las Vegas is as uniquely American as hamburgers, Arnold Schwarzenegger action movies and cheesy tabloid television shows. While we may not want to admit it, these are all things most of us find appealing — at least covertly.

In recent years, Las Vegas has even begun to live up to its own hype as an adult "Disneyland" with the advent of the so-called "mega-resorts:" hotel-casinos that take a particular theme to its most elaborate and, frequently, exaggerated extremes.

So now we have the "Mirage," with its 30-foot manmade volcano, white tigers, dolphin tanks and "Siegfried and Roy" magic extravaganza, as well as "Excalibur," a King Arthur and the Knights of the Roundtable-themed hotel-casino and the "Wizard of Oz"-influenced "MGM" hotel and theme park.

Las Vegas has become a resort destination like Orlando and Los Angeles — but with better weather and cheaper parking. Along the way, it has also acquired other attractions, some small, some large, that help make it a fun place to visit, even if you don't want to gamble.

These other places include historic sites, such as the Mormon Fort, and more than a half-dozen museums, ranging from the sublime (the Nevada State Historical Society and Museum) to the esoteric (Liberace Museum).

Additionally, contrary to some views, southern Nevada consists of more than simply Las Vegas. It has quaint, historic communities, such as Boulder City, and booming border resort towns, such as Laughlin.

Of course, none of what you're about to read is intended to be an all-inclusive view of what you can do in southern Nevada. Rather, these are a handful of the more intriguing, entertaining or interesting places found there.

Join me in exploring the other side of southern Nevada — the man-made attractions found in the Neon Desert.

Historic Las Vegas

BELIEVE IT OR NOT, Las Vegas has history.

To prove the point, the Preservation Association of Clark County has developed an historic pamphlet debunking the myth that the oldest thing in Las Vegas is yesterday's copy of the "Racing News."

The brochure offers information about two dozen historic buildings and sites in the Las Vegas area. While it is true that much of the original Las Vegas has disappeared over the years to accommodate the city's rapid growth, there are a few "old-timers" around that provide a glimpse into the city's rich past.

Ironically, since Las Vegas is generally perceived as a "new" western city, the name, which is Spanish for "the meadows," is one of the oldest place names in the state. Records indicate that in the late 1820s and 1830s, traders on the Old Spanish Trail often camped there in meadows fed by natural springs.

Later in 1844, explorer John C. Fremont camped in the locale. It was his descriptions of the area that attracted later travelers, including many settlers who used it as a watering spot on their journey to California.

The oldest remaining building in Las Vegas is the Old Mormon Fort, located at 908 Las Vegas Boulevard North. Here you can see the last remaining structure of a complex of adobe buildings built by Mormon colonists in 1855. Tours of the simple adobe building on the fort site, now a small museum, are offered daily in the summer.

The Mormon settlement was not a success and was abandoned in 1858. A few years later, the fort site was rebuilt and became the heart of the Las Vegas Ranch, established by Octavius D. Gass.

The ranch flourished for the rest of the century under not only Gass (who owned it until 1881) but later owners. In 1902, the ranch was sold to the Union Pacific Railroad, which extended its line to Las Vegas in 1905. That same year, the modern town of Las Vegas was surveyed and started by the railroad.

The railroad was a major influence on Las Vegas. Many of the older buildings in the city date from this period, including the Railroad Storehouse Building at 700 Dividend Drive (also called Hanson Hall), built in 1910 and the Victory Hotel at 307 N. Main Street, built the same year, which is the oldest remaining downtown hotel.

Later, the beginning of construction of Hoover Dam in 1930, which attracted hundreds of workers to the area, created a new boom in Las Vegas. While some felt completion of the dam would cause Las Vegas to revert to its previous status as a sleepy railroad town in the desert, another development, the legalization of gambling in 1931, pushed Las Vegas into a fast lane.

The Las Vegas brochure lists a number of other interesting historic buildings, such as:

- The Post Office/Federal Building at 301 E. Stewart, constructed in 1933 in the neo-classical style popular for government buildings at the time. Big and impressive, this building, like Hoover Dam, is a good example of the simple yet elegant federal architecture of the 30's.

- The El Portal Theater at 310 E. Fremont, built in 1928, which was the city's first modern movie house.

- Las Vegas High School at 315 S. Seventh, built in 1931 and restored a few years ago,.which is the city's only remaining example of the Art Deco architecture of the 1930s. This is a truly beautiful structure with its intricate terra cotta facing.

- The Hitching Post Wedding Chapel at 226 Las Vegas Blvd. S., built as a residence in 1923, then converted to a chapel in 1934. This is one of the city's earliest and most tasteful wedding chapels.

Of course, no historic brochure about Las Vegas could overlook the importance of the gaming industry to the city's development. One of the oldest survivors from the city's early gaming industry is the giant "Vegas Vic" neon sign in front of the Pioneer Casino at 25 E. Fremont in downtown Las Vegas. "Vic," who was erected in 1951, was for many years the symbol of the Las Vegas Chamber of Commerce.

To receive a free copy of the Preservation Association of Clark County's brochure, "A Guide to Historic Las Vegas," send a self-addressed, stamped envelope to the Nevada State Museum at 700 Twin Lakes Blvd., Las Vegas, NV 89158. ❧

7   *Las Vegas*
         High School

Nevada State Museum, Las Vegas

Southern Nevada's
History on Display

A PAIR OF BROWN GEESE waddle across a patch of green lawn and slide into a large pond. Tall, mature trees cast cool shadows over a young couple picnicking on the grass adjacent to the pond.

In this peaceful setting — a place called Lorenzi Park — it's hard to believe you're only a few miles away, and not a world away, from the glitz and glamour of the nearby Las Vegas Strip.

It is here you'll find the Nevada State Museum and Historical Society, the southern Nevada branch of the state museum system. Founded in 1982, the facility offers several permanent exhibits that reveal more than ten thousand years of local and regional history, as well as changing galleries.

The museum is located at 700 Twin Lakes Drive. To reach it from downtown Las Vegas, travel north on U.S. Highway 95 (toward Tonopah), then turn right on Exit 78 (Valley View Exit). Turn right on Bonanza Road and head straight to the museum.

Entering the museum, housed in an attractive Spanish-style building with tan stucco walls and a red-tile roof, the first room is the Hall of Biological Science. Here, are exhibits describing the geology, plant and animal life of the Great Basin region, of which Nevada is a part.

A large bighorn sheep stands in a diorama in the center of the room, a proud and appropriate symbol of the Great Basin. Wall panels are divided into several displays featuring different aspects of the development and history of the area.

For example, one panel describes the Spring Mountain Range as a "biological island," because of the wide variety of plant and animal life found within this relatively compact biological system. Others explain the pinon-juniper community, the creosote brush community and the black brush community, complete with animals in the context of those surroundings.

Adjacent to the Hall of Biological Science is a rotating gallery, which, during a recent visit, featured "World War II and the Emergence of Modern Las Vegas." This fascinating exhibit incorporated vintage photos of the emerging Las Vegas, including scenes of the Flamingo Hotel, the first major hotel-casino on the famed Strip, which was built following the war.

Another gallery features changing art exhibits. Recent shows have included the photography of Stephen Trimble, who has taken extensive shots of the Great Basin region, including some wonderful views of Wheeler Peak in eastern Nevada and the Ruby Mountains of northeastern Nevada.

In the hallway, another photograph display shows historic scenes of Las Vegas, focusing on residential neighborhoods in the 1930s.

The Hall of Regional History, on the western end of the building, is the largest, and in my mind, most interesting room in the museum. Here, visitors can trace the history of southern Nevada, starting with remains of early man found at Tule Springs (now part of the Floyd Lamb State Park).

Archaeologists have found a variety of fossils at Tule Springs, including a mammoth tusk and jawbone. It is the site of the earliest recorded presence of man in Nevada.

Another display describes the Anasazi (or "ancient ones"), which were a native American culture that thrived until about 1150 A.D. A companion exhibit discusses the Lost City and Mesa House Period (700-1150 A.D.).

Other displays feature the Spanish Trail, a trade route between Santa Fe and Los Angeles, originally blazed by Spanish explorers in the 1700s, as well as the "Mountain Men," such as Peter Skene Ogden and Kit Carson, who explored Nevada's interior in the mid-19th century.

A large freight wagon in the middle of the room towers over the displays and is an historic relic of the Emigrant Period, during which hundreds of settlers traveled across Nevada on their way to California and Oregon.

The historical records continue through the advent of the railroads in the state, the Mormon settlement period, the construction of Hoover Dam, the mining booms, legalized gambling and the testing of the Atomic bomb in the deserts of southern Nevada in the 1950s).

The museum also offers a fine library of books, maps, manuscripts, indexes and photographs related to the history of both the state and the Las Vegas area. Called the Cahlan Library, these materials are available to researchers during museum hours.

Admission to the museum is $2 for adults, children under 18 free. It is open daily from 8:30 a.m. to 4:30 p.m. (except for Thanksgiving Day, Christmas Day and New Year's Day). A small gift shop near the entryway offers a nice selection of Nevada posters and books. For more information, contact the Nevada State Museum, 700 Twin Lakes Drive, Las Vegas, NV 89107, (702) 486-5205. ❧

Liberace Museum

A Tribute to
"Mr. Showmanship"

NEW YORK has the Metropolitan Museum of Art, Paris has the Louvre and Las Vegas has — the Liberace Museum.

Only in glitter city can you find a museum dedicated to the late, often controversial pianist, Wladziu Valentino Liberace, aka "Mr. Showmanship."

Celebrating the outrageous, "kitsch" style of Liberace, the museum is quite interesting. For instance, where else can you see the world's largest rhinestone — 23 kilograms in weight, 310-by-230mm in size and worth about $50,000? Or a pair of stuffed hound dogs that were a gift from Colonel Tom Parker, who was Elvis' manager?

The museum is jam-packed with unusual and often bizarre items once owned by the entertainer who made candelabras a household word.

In many ways the museum is a shrine to Liberace — from the piano-shaped reception desk to the wax figurines of the man dressed in the always-extravagant outfits that were his trademark.

The collection has a number of Liberace's famous capes, including a few lined with mink and other exotic furs. Of course, the man had an absolute fetish for things that sparkled and, as a result, there are dozens of bejeweled stage costumes. The museum estimates that the costumes alone are worth more than $1 million dollars.

In addition to clothes, the entertainer collected rare pianos and fine cars. Among the pianos are those played by Liszt, Schumann and Brahms and George Gershwin's Chickering grand piano. In addition to the class pianos, there are also a few that were unique to Liberace, including two mirror-tiled Baldwins and a rhinestone-studded model.

His auto collection, on display, included a gold-flaked Bradley GT, a Durham-designed Cadillac limousine with built-in television, and bar and a red, white and blue Rolls-Royce with only 900 miles on the odometer — most of which was logged during his 1976 Bicentennial salute at the Las Vegas Hilton.

Some of the more bizarre items are a gold mold of Liberace's hands, a fur-lined violin and a mosaic portrait in sequins (naturally), made by one of his adoring fans.

The walls of the museum are lined with framed awards and commendations as well as family photographs, newspaper clippings, performance handbills and a life-size oil painting of Liberace.

The museum was created as a non-profit endeavor to raise funds for the Liberace Foundation for the Performing and Creative Arts and all proceeds from admission provide the foundation with money for music scholarships at 22 schools and colleges.

The Liberace Museum is located at 1775 E. Tropicana Avenue in Las Vegas. Admission (actually a donation) is $3.50 for adults, $3 for seniors, $2 for children under 12 accompanied by an adult. The museum is open daily from 10 a.m. to 5 p.m., Sundays from 1 p.m. to 5 p.m. For more information, call (702) 798-5595. ❧

Recapturing a "Sense of Wonder"

AN EIGHT-YEAR-OLD GIRL steps onto a concrete circle, surrounded by a two-inch-wide trough filled with soapy liquid, and pulls on an overhead rope. A circular plastic pipe, connected to the rope, slowly rises from the liquid and forms a massive bubble tube around the now-giggling girl.

Meanwhile, across the room, a ten-year-old boy sits before a panel of blinking lights, switches and steering controls and frantically attempts to correct the wobbly flight of a four-foot model of a space shuttle, hanging overhead.

Welcome to the wonders of the Lied Discovery Children's Museum in Las Vegas. Since opening in 1990, the museum has challenged, charmed and captivated thousands of children with its more than 130 hands-on exhibits spread over 40,000 square feet of space.

Located north of downtown Las Vegas, across North Las Vegas Boulevard from Cashman Field (home of the Las Vegas Stars, a minor-league professional baseball team), the Lied Museum is one of the new brand of children-oriented museums opening in cities across the country.

Arriving at the Lied Museum, it's pretty obvious this is something different from a traditional museum. The design of the exterior of the building incorporates various shapes — a large, round tower, a cone, rectangles and squares — that resemble giant versions of a child's building blocks.

Inside, the museum is divided into nearly two dozen "themed" areas, including, "Places and Spaces," "Bubbles," "Communications," "Music," "Visual Arts," "Human Performance," "Everyday Living," "Science Principles," "The Number Place," "What Can I Be?" and "Discovery Radio Station."

Within each of these broad categories, there are individual exhibits, each designed to illustrate and demonstrate those themes in ways that are both fun and informative (but certainly don't let any kid know it's "educational").

For example, the area called "Everyday Living" contains a handful of intriguing displays designed to show children how to develop some of the skills required to survive in our modern society. "The Lied Discovery Store" is a replica of a grocery store, complete with make-believe products. Shoppers wander the aisles, picking up a wide variety of groceries, then take them to a checkout stand, complete with electronic cash register, which can also be operated by the child.

Adjacent to the store is the "Lied Discovery Bank," a replica of a bank that features an automatic teller machine and a teller window (where a museum volunteer can answer any questions). Next to the bank is the "Lied Discovery Mail," a replica of a post office.

In the "Bubbles" section, kids can learn how bubbles work with the "Bubble Tube" (described at the beginning of this column) as well as a display called, "Bubble Art," at which the child blows into a sheet of soapy liquid and forms different size and colors of bubbles.

One of the most popular attractions is the "KKID, Discovery Radio Station," at which participants can play disc jockey, select-

Lied Discovery Children's Museum

ing musical cartridges to play and speaking on a microphone — both of which are heard throughout the museum, making everyone there your audience.

Another crowded exhibit is the wheelchair basketball game. The object of this display is to show kids what it would be like if they couldn't do something most of them take for granted.

And still another popular display is the infirmary, where the children can play with "Stuffee," a giant cotton, stuffed doll whose front can be unzipped to reveal his internal workings. While it sounds strange, kids can "feel" simplified versions of his heart, stomach, intestines and other organs — and learn about anatomy.

Wandering through the museum, it's easy to find something of interest (even if you're an adult). Over here, you're stepping on large pads marked with musical notes, attempting to play a tune (kind of like the big keyboard in the movie, "Big"), while over there, you're standing in a strangely glowing room looking at your shadow, which has been flashed on walls made of photo sensitive material (don't worry, it fades after a few minutes).

Of special note are the changing workshops conducted daily at the museum, which can include subjects such as masking making, cartooning and other topics.

In addition to the two floors of museum exhibits and demonstrations, the facility also includes the snack bar called "Stuffee's Place," a well-stocked gift store and a branch of the Las Vegas Library system.

The museum is located at 833 Las Vegas Boulevard North, Las Vegas, NV 89101. Hours are Tuesday, Thursday, Friday and Saturday, 10 a.m. to 5 p.m.; Wednesday, 10 a.m. to 7 p.m.; Sunday, 12 noon to 5 p.m.; closed on Mondays. Admission is $4 for adults, $2.50 for seniors and children 12 and older, $1.50 for children 11 to 4, free for children 3 and under. Group tours and special birthday programs are available. For information, call (702) 382-3445. ❧

Fish, Fowl,
Fur and Fangs

A MASSIVE WHITE SHARK hangs from the ceiling, its huge partially-open mouth dwarfing a bearded man who inspects the dozens of large, sharp teeth half-hidden inside. He shakes his head slightly, as if imagining what it would be like to face this creature of the sea on its turf, and moves on to study the shark's smaller cousins, about a dozen of which are also on display on surrounding walls.

The setting is the Las Vegas Natural History Museum, one of the newest additions to the southern Nevada cultural scene. Opened in 1991, the museum is another example of the recent efforts throughout the state to develop educationally-oriented family attractions.

The Las Vegas Natural History Museum is located at 900 Las Vegas Boulevard North, adjacent to Cashman Field and the historic Mormon Fort, and across the street from the Lied Discovery Children's Museum.

Situated in the former home of the Las Vegas Elks Club, the Natural History Museum offers a variety of exhibits displaying animals, insects, aquatic life and other aspects of nature.

In addition to the Great White, the Shark Room contains examples of other, no less imposing species, including the colorful Tiger shark, the Mako shark and the unusual Hammerhead shark. Tanks at the entrance to the room contain two small living sharks, a Catshark and Leopard shark, both of which visitors can help feed at different times of the day.

An informative video tells the story of these frequently misunderstood fish — "Jaws" didn't do them any favors. But lest you feel too sorry for them, a display case shows some of the things found inside sharks, ranging from California license plates to a hubcap. Another exhibit features some of the products made from sharks.

Adjacent to the Shark exhibit is the World Wildlife Room, which contains several dozen mounted animals on display. Here, you can find lions, cheetahs, pumas, antelopes, tigers, a huge upright polar bear, and a wide variety of wolves, birds and other animals.

The hallway gallery offers an opportunity to view one of the world's largest and best collections of wood carved birds. These marvelously realistic works, include beautiful representations of eagles and a wonderful macaw.

For those into bugs, the Flight Room focuses on birds, bats and plenty of flying insects. Here, you'll find an exquisite butterfly collection as well as preserved spiders, hawks, owls and various raptors.

Of special note is the collection of various types of eggs. Accumulated in 1910, this collection is irreplaceable since it is illegal today to collect eggs.

Children will find the "Hands On Room" particularly interesting with its "dig-a-fossil" display (kids can dig through sand for different kinds of replica fossil bones and artifacts) and the samples of dinosaur bones, which they can touch.

A left-over from the dinosaur exhibit is the Fossil Room, attached to the Shark Room, which contains a diorama exhibit of a "Parasaurolophus" (a small duck-billed creature) and a "Saurorinthoides," a small bird-like dinosaur. Other displays feature actual bones of a prehistoric bison, the jaw bone of a "Phobosuchus," and the remains of a "Dunkleosteus," a large, armored fish.

A well-stocked gift store offers visitors a chance to take home their own plastic thunder lizards or stuffed shark. It also contains a nice collection of natural history books.

While the museum is still in its formative stages, immediate plans include completion of an expansion of the "Hands On" room and development of other exhibits. Additionally, the city of Las Vegas has prepared a master plan for the area, which would be converted into a series of museums and research facilities.

In the future, there will be a Las Vegas Neon Museum, a wild collection of many of the city's outrageous and unusual casino signs — many of which are now considered historical. The plans also calls for a permanent archeological dig exhibit on the site of the nearby Mormon Fort, the first settlement in the Las Vegas Valley.

The Las Vegas Natural History Museum is open daily 9 a.m. to 4 p.m. Admission is $5 for adults, $4 for seniors and military, $2.50 for children 4-12 and free for children under 4. For more information, contact (702) 384-3466. ✺

Las Vegas Museum of Natural History

Guinness World of Records Museum
(Photo courtesy of
Guinness World of Records Museum)

Amazing Guinness

DURING THE PAST FEW YEARS, one of the biggest changes to occur in Las Vegas — in addition to the huge influx of people — has been the growth in non-gaming attractions.

One of the newest is the Guinness World of Records Museum located at 2780 Las Vegas Boulevard South on the famed Strip, adjacent to the Circus Circus Hotel-Casino.

Opened in 1990, the 5,200 square foot Guinness Museum is the three-dimensional version of the famous Book of World Records with life-size replicas, videos and other displays detailing the tallest, shortest, biggest, longest and most outrageous things in the world.

For instance, imagine a man weighing 1,069 pounds, a woman with 95 percent of her body covered with tattoos or the world's record for eating raw oysters — all have been certified as authentic and are featured in the Guinness Museum.

The displays have all been designed to make them interactive. In some areas this involves computers that answer questions about world records in sports or music. In other exhibits, visitors are invited to see how they measure up to the biggest and smallest.

The first exhibit relates the story of Robert Pershing Wadlow, the world's tallest man at 8 feet, 11 inches. Film from the 1940s shows Wadlow walking, speaking and being measured to determine his growth rate. In keeping with the participatory nature of the museum, visitors can stand next to the replica of Wadlow (I reached his waist).

Nearby is a display showing Robert Earl Hughes, one of the heaviest men in the history of the world. In 1958, Hughes weighed 1,069 pounds. Across the way is a representation of Shigechiyo Izumi, who died in 1986 at the official age of 120 years, 237 days — the world's oldest recorded human.

One of the more unusual exhibits is one showing videos of various eating records. In full color (complete with realistic and disgusting sound), you can watch the world's records broken for consuming spaghetti, grapes, eggs and other fare.

Another film shows the world's greatest shallow dives — Henri La Mothe jumped from a height of 28 feet into a 12-inch wading pool — while a photo display tells the story of Roy C. Sullivan, the "human lightning rod," who survived seven lightning strikes.

Following the exhibits of weird personal records, called the Human World, the museum is divided into several displays highlighting records in sports, entertainment, space and the animal kingdom.

In the World of Sports area, computerized data banks challenge visitors to guess records in everything from boxing to football, soccer to baseball. The Animal World features computer displays about the oldest monkey, the most poisonous fish and other denizens of the wild kingdom.

Another area depicts space achievements, including historic film footage of space flights, astronauts, cosmonauts and moon explorations. Nature's Wonders highlights incredible wonderlands like the Grand Canyon (largest canyon) and Death Valley (lowest point on earth).

Judging by the crowd, the most popular part of the museum is the World of Cinema and Arts & Entertainment sections. Here visitors can find out about the world's most recorded songs, biggest seller, longest record on the U.S. and United Kingdom charts (believe it or not, Meatloaf's "Bat Out of Hell" holds the U.K. record with 391 consecutive weeks on the charts).

In a nod to glitter city, the museum also has displays showing some of the world records related to that community. For example, Las Vegas is the largest city in the U.S. that was founded in this century, while the Palace Station Casino holds the record for world's largest free-standing electronic sign.

Admission to the Guinness Museum is $4.95 for adults, $3.95 for seniors, military and students while the cost is $2.95 for children. The museum is open daily from 9 a.m. to 9 p.m., Sunday through Thursday, 9 a.m. to 10 p.m., Friday and Saturday. For more information, call (702) 792-3766. ᰤ

Ripley's Believe It or Not! Museum
(Photo courtesy of
Four Queens Hotel and Casino)

Believe It Or Not!
At Ripley's

THE RIPLEY'S BELIEVE IT OR NOT! MUSEUM in downtown Las Vegas is a virtual celebration of all that is weird, strange and offbeat in the world.

Located inside the Four Queens Hotel and Casino, at 202 East Fremont Street, the 9,100-square-foot museum is the largest of nine similar museums in the United States that contain hundreds of weird and exotic artifacts from the famous Robert Ripley collection.

Ripley was a nationally-syndicated newspaper cartoonist (the Believe It or Not! column continues to appear in hundreds of newspapers), who specialized in writing and drawing about the bizarre, the rare and the unusual.

During his lifetime, he also collected millions of unusual objects that became fodder for his cartoons and, after his death in 1949, the basis for the Ripley museums found in England, Canada and the United States.

Since opening in 1986, the Las Vegas Ripley's museum has intrigued thousands of visitors who can't help but be fascinated by this Smithsonian of the strange. When you enter, you quickly realize that this isn't your ordinary museum; each room has been designed to enhance the mood of the displays.

For instance, stalactites hang eerily from the ceiling of the chamber devoted to exhibits featuring torture devices and famous, macabre deaths. This is not a place for the squeamish with its cave-like appearance and the soft screams of imaginary victims filtering through the background.

You can wander for hours exploring all the displays and reading all the stories behind the objects in the museum. One room displaying African artifacts has a decidedly jungle motif, complete with beating drums and a grass hut. In another room, you can find a two-headed calf (now stuffed, but a video shows it was alive) or a man with a horn growing out of his head.

Another exhibit shows a log cabin built out of nearly 10,000 Lincoln pennies, while there are wax figures of the world's tallest man, the world's biggest glutton — he spent $250,000 per meal while his poor mother starved to death — and of a Chinese nobleman born with double pupils in each eye.

You can also learn about the "Lighthouse Man," who wandered the streets of Chungking, China with a lighted candle stuck in a hole in his head, find a replica of the London Tower Bridge made from 264,345 matchsticks or view an authentic Iron Maiden, certainly one of the most ominous torture devices ever created.

It's all pretty strange and fascinating — and worth a visit.

The Ripley's museum is open 9 a.m. to midnight Sunday through Thursday and 9 a.m. to 1 a.m. Friday and Saturday. For more more information, call (702) 385-4011. ❧

Wet n' Wild
Summer Fun

WHEN THE TEMPERATURES begin hovering in the 90s, it's as good a time as any to visit one of the absolutely coolest places in the state — the Wet n' Wild water theme park in Las Vegas.

With more than 26 acres of pools, tubes, canels, slides, waterways and water cannons, Wet n' Wild delights and refreshes visitors to the hot southern Nevada environs. Located on the world famous Las Vegas Strip, the park is open from mid-April to late September.

Like nearly everything in Las Vegas, Wet n' Wild has a larger than life quality. It boasts the fastest and highest water chute in the world, called Der Stuka, because, say the folks at W & W, the rider falls almost straight down, like the World War II German dive bomber.

Der Stuka is der scary. Actually, the climb up a circular walkway to 76-feet above the park is the worst part since the ride down is over in seconds. At the top, you are urged to lie on your back with your arms and feet crossed (in a kind of modified praying position for those hoping to survive the ride).

At the top, an attendant gently shoves you down the water slide. On my way down, I tried to keep my eyes open, watching the blur of glittery neon signs as I plummeted down the slide into a pool of water. Needless to say, this is not a ride for the faint of heart.

Other favorites include the Banzai Boggan, a water roller coaster in which you ride atop a plastic sled, down a sharp incline, then skim across a 120-foot pool (the trick seems to be to try to keep your balance and ride the sled without falling off of it into the water).

Another good ride is the Raging Rapids, on which you ride an inner tube on a 500-foot long river complete with whirlpools, waterfalls and rapids. Who needs to raft the Colorado when you have all of this?

For the adventurous, there are Whitewater Slideways (three dizzying, twisting water slides dropping from 50-feet in the air) and the Hydra-Maniac (a twisting, turning, gut-wrenching series of spiral water tubes).

Those seeking more leisurely entertainment will find that the park offers a Suntan Lagoon and the Lazy River, which is a ribbon of water with a slight two-mile an hour current that runs around the park and allows you to drift along on a raft or inner tube.

For the younger set, the park has a Children's Water Playground with a 1930s style Zepplin for climbing and a variety of water cannons and squirting devices. There is also a 500,000 gallon Surf Lagoon with real waves that is perfect for smaller children and those seeking a rest.

Each year, Wet n' Wild tries to introduce new rides, designed to keep things new and fresh. In recent years, additions have included the Blue Niagra, which transports you through more than 300-feet in two intertwining, looping water tubes. The sensation is incredible as you wind through the curled plastic tubes, seemingly forever.

There is also the Bubble-Up, a giant colorful bubble with cascading water pouring from the top. The effect is of climbing, slipping and sliding on a massive beach ball.

Open 10 a.m. to 6 p.m. in spring and fall, 10 a.m. to 8 p.m. summer. Admission to the park is $15.95 for adults, $12.95 for children. For more information, contact Wet n' Wild, 2601 Las Vegas Boulevard South, Las Vegas, NV 89109, (702) 737-7873. ❧

Wet n' Wild
(Photo courtesy of
Las Vegas News Bureau)

31

Ethel M Cactus Gardens
(Photo courtesy of
Las Vegas News Bureau)

Chocolate Heaven

LONG SUFFERING "CHOCOHOLICS" should skip this chapter.

The rest of you, who find your way into the industrial part of Henderson in southern Nevada, will find the Ethel M plant is a combination of candy manufacturing facility and cactus garden that is, without a doubt, Nevada's sweetest attraction.

As a dedicated choco-connoisseur, naturally I decided to start off my tour of the place with dessert. Now anyone who has ever appreciated fine chocolate knows the name Ethel M. Owned by the Mars candy family (M & M's, Mars Bars, Snickers, etc.), Ethel M is their upscale chocolate label that is generally only available in specialty shops in shopping malls and airports.

When Ethel M chocolates first appeared a few years ago, they were particularly unique because they were filled with liqueur creams, including Amaretto, Bourbon and Creme de Menthe (my favorite). The booze-flavored fillings are an interesting gimmick, but the candy has gained fans because of the excellent quality of the chocolate.

During a short tour of the state-of-the-art candy plant, a recorded message explains that Ethel M uses a special formula to make its gourmet chocolate. While technically a milk chocolate, Ethel M's chocolate incorporates many of the characteristics and flavors associated with dark chocolate. According to the company, this process results in a richer, more flavorful chocolate.

Over the years, while the liqueur chocolates have continued to be popular, Ethel M has broadened its product line to include other items, such as chocolate coins (sold in clever packages to resemble slot machines) and outrageously tasty truffles.

The best part of the Ethel M Chocolate Factory tour is the end, where you are deposited in a gift shop and given your choice of a free chocolate. The choices are difficult but no one is a loser — and if you can't make up your mind, purchase a sampler to take home.

Outside of the factory, Ethel M has developed a two-and-a-half acre Cactus Garden exhibiting more than 350 different species of cactus, succulents and desert plants from the southwest and various deserts throughout the world.

To a non-cactus expert, this place seems like a prickly Garden of Eden. You can find a wide variety of plants ranging from Beavertail and Purple Pancake Prickly Pears to Golden Barrels and Sahuaros.

The Ethel M Chocolate Factory and Cactus Garden is located seven miles from the Las Vegas Strip. Drive 5.5 miles east of the Strip on Tropicana Avenue to Mountain Vista. Turn right on Mountain Vista and drive 2 miles to Sunset Way (past the factory). Turn left at the traffic light into Green Valley Business Park, then left again on to Cactus Garden Drive.

The factory and gardens are open daily from 9 a.m. to 5:30 p.m. Admission is free. Special guided tours are offered at 9:30, 10:30, 11:30, 1:30 and 3:30. For information, call (702) 458-8864. ✺

Life Before
Bugsy

THERE'S A POPULAR MYTH that nothing existed in Southern Nevada before Benjamin "Bugsy" Siegel built the original Flamingo Hotel in 1947 near a sleepy desert hamlet called Las Vegas.

While it is certainly true the Flamingo introduced big time gambling to Nevada and helped put Las Vegas on the map, a visit to the Clark County Heritage Museum in Henderson proves there was life before Bugsy.

One of the first things you notice about the museum is the amount of space it encompasses. Located on an open stretch of 20 acres, the museum has plenty of room to display the considerable history of the region.

The main museum building is the restored Boulder City Depot, which originally served passengers on the Union Pacific spur from Las Vegas to Boulder City. Built in 1931, the depot was relocated to the museum property in 1976 and has served as the museum headquarters since 1979.

A Union Pacific caboose and railcar, restored to original working condition, are parked adjacent to the depot, giving the place the appearance of still being in use.

Inside the depot, you'll find exhibits ranging from fossils of prehistoric sea life and dinosaurs that once roamed the area to ancient tools and handmade baskets created by Southern Nevada's original inhabitants.

The museum also contains a rotating gallery that features special exhibits. Past shows have spotlighted such subjects as the history of neon in Las Vegas and Native American basketry. A depot gift shop offers a variety of souvenirs and books about Nevada and the west.

Adjacent to the depot, is Heritage Street, a row of restored historic homes and buildings representing various eras in Southern Nevada's past. To date, a half-dozen buildings have been moved to Heritage Street and returned to original condition with period furnishings. Entering any of the structures triggers a recorded self-guided tour.

The oldest building is the Giles/Barcus House, a home originally built in the mining town of Goldfield in 1906, then moved to Las Vegas in the early 1950s. It served as a residence, then was used as a retail store.

Next door is the Beckley House, built in 1912 by Will Beckley, a pioneer Las Vegas businessman. The California-style bungalow is representative of the type of homes common in Las Vegas during the first few decades of this century.

Townsite House is representative of the kind of "company town" homes constructed in the 1940s to house workers at the giant Basic Magnesium plant in Henderson.

Across the way is the Tudor-influenced Heritage/P.J. Goumond House, which was similar to many of the larger homes built in Las Vegas in the 1930s by one of the state's earliest gaming pioneers.

Another structure is a replica of a 19th century newspaper office, complete with authentic turn-of-the-century newspaper presses and equipment.

As with much of Nevada, the Las Vegas area was originally settled by farmers, then miners. The museum has an interpretive trail that winds through displays of antique mining equipment and leads to the remains of a Nevada ghost town.

The ghost town consists of genuine 19th century mining shacks and businesses that have been moved to the site from other mining camps.

The trail also leads to a replica of a prehistoric Nevada Paiute Indian camp that includes examples of grass and pole lodgings, hunting tools and other artifacts.

An excellent book describing Las Vegas' early years is "Las Vegas, As It Began, As It Grew," by Stanley W. Paher (same author of the equally well-done book, "Nevada Ghost Towns and Mining Camps").

The Clark County Heritage Museum is located 10 miles from downtown Las Vegas at 1830 South Boulder Highway. The museum is open Monday through Friday from 8 a.m. to 5 p.m., Saturday and Sunday from 9 a.m. to 5 p.m. Admission is $1 for adults and 50 cents for children and seniors. For more information, contact the museum at (702) 565-0907. ❧

*Clark County
Heritage Museum*

Boulder City

Nevada's
Garden City

BOULDER CITY IS DIFFERENT from most Nevada communities. For one things, it's green. Really green. Boasting tall trees, lush parks, immaculate brick homes and a downtown section filled with striking 1930s commercial architecture, Boulder City has retained its unique flavor as America's first planned community.

The town owes its existence (and its greenness) to nearby Hoover Dam. Work began on the dam in 1931 and, shortly after, builders began setting up shelters on the townsite.

Historic records indicate that identifying an actual "birthdate" for Boulder City is difficult since buildings and homes were erected before the actual townsite was established.

However, a number of significant events occurred in the first year, including the opening of the Boulder City train station on January 4, 1930, the driving of the first stake in the ground by surveyors on March 16, 1931, and the opening of the post office on April 15, 1931.

An official townsite map was completed on May 26 of that year and marked the true birth of Boulder City. The map plan was thorough and complete. The federal government, which developed Boulder City, envisioned a community of 5,000 people, and determined everything from the types of business that would be allowed to the kinds of trees that would be planted.

The map was unique. Buildings were arranged in a kind of fan pattern, spreading out from the Reclamation Administration Building (the dam's headquarters), which was located on a hill north of town. Residential neighborhoods were rectangular, sidewalks constructed around the perimeter and alleys down the center.

The town design also featured several parks, including the large Government Park in the center of the community. It is this greenery that makes Boulder City so special. Considerable thought went into the development of the parks. A landscaper was hired by the federal government — named, appropriately, Wilbur Weed.

Weed studied the desert soil and worked with landscape architects from other dry areas to determine that there were several types of trees that could thrive, including elms, poplars, cypresses, sycamores and evergreens. Other than a rose garden that never quite survived (and was removed in the first year), Weed's handiwork continues to be found throughout the city.

In addition to the beautiful (green) landscaping, Boulder City has a number of well preserved buildings and homes. One of the best examples of the city's 1930s architecture is the Boulder City Hotel, constructed in 1933.

The hotel, located in the middle of the town, has long been one of the centerpieces of the community. Built to accommodate all the tourists watching construction of the dam, the two-story Dutch Colonial building originally included an elegant paneled lobby and 33 guest rooms with private tiled baths.

Early guests included a number of celebrities, including comedian Harold Lloyd, actor Ronald Coleman and the Maharajah and Maharanee of Indore, India.

The hotel was expanded over the years, adding another 48 rooms and a large dining room. The tourism business began to decline during World War II, when gas became scarce, and the hotel entered a period of decline. In 1980, an investment group restored the old hotel, however, reestablishing its reputation as one of the finest inns in the west.

A walk through the (green) tree-lined streets of Boulder City reveals other architectural gems, including the art deco movie theatre, the majestic red-brick municipal building and a number of churches and homes. In keeping with the historic, 1930s ambience, the new city office building incorporates a brick facade and blends well with the rest of the town.

The town also maintains a busy schedule of special events each year, including several art shows (the town has an active artist community). The oldest is the annual Art in the Park show in October, while there is also the Spring Jamboree and Artisans Fair and the Clark County Artist Show held in May.

An informative book on the development of Boulder City, available at local shops, is "In the Beginning," a history of Boulder City by Dennis McBride. Additionally, the Boulder City Visitors Bureau and Museum in the downtown district features free showings of an excellent movie describing the construction of Hoover Dam and Boulder City. The museum also offers souvenirs, gifts and a snack shop.

For information, contact the Visitors Bureau at (702) 293-1823 or the Boulder City Chamber of Commerce, (702) 293-2034. ❧

Hoover Dam

Hoover Dam
Calms the Colorado

HOOVER DAM does its job well.

From the moment you first see it, you have no doubt this massive sheet of gray concrete can tame the mighty Colorado River and will probably do so forever.

The dam was conceived in the 1920s as a way to finally control the Colorado River, which habitually flooded much of the fertile farmland in southern California. Work began in 1931 and the structure was completed in 1935 — two years ahead of schedule.

Hoover Dam may one of the few times the hyperbole matches the reality. It has been called one of the seven architectural wonders of the world and easily lives up to its billing.

This is one huge dam. While a handful of newer dams may be larger — Hoover is now the third highest in the world — you have o remember that this dam was built more than a half century ago, ring America's Great Depression.

Despite its age, the statistics about the dam remain staggering.

The dam cost $175 million dollars and contains 3.25 million cubic yards of concrete, which is enough to pave a two-lane highway from San Francisco to New York. It measures 726.4 feet high and 1,244 feet across.

The waters of the Colorado that are held back by the dam form Lake Mead, which is the largest manmade reservoir in the world.

While it appears to look like a giant curved curtain, the dam is actually shaped more like a huge upside-down wedge, with a base in the bedrock that is 660 feet thick. It's darn difficult not to be impressed when you stand at the top and look 528 feet straight down to the Colorado River.

Engineers point out that Hoover Dam was "overbuilt," meaning it contains far more concrete and metal support than is actually necessary to do its job. But that's what makes it so impressive and has assured that the dam is built to last — perhaps for centuries.

Guided tours of the dam are given every few minutes and more than 26 million people have toured the dam since it opened in 1935. The 35-minute tour begins at the top and within seconds you drop in an elevator the full 500-plus feet to the base.

Inside the dam you can find small architectural touches that make it so unique. Because it was built in the 1930s, the designers incorporated art deco designs into the structure. For instance, there are stylized Native American designs in the floor tiles.

At the base you tour a massive chamber filled with 17 power generators that supply more than 1 million kilowatts of electricity. From there, you can also walk deep inside the dam to see the huge diversion tunnels that were built to divert the river water around the dam during construction.

Once back at the top, you can head northwest to the Nevada side (the dam bridges Nevada and Arizona) to the Welcome Center and gift shop. Exhibits at the center describe the entire

Colorado River water system — how it starts and where it ends — and the history of the dam.

Additionally, be sure to check out the striking winged bronze sculptures that stand adjacent to the dam. Entitled "Winged Figures of the Republic," the work was designed by Oskar J.W. Hansen and are believed to be the largest monumental bronzes ever cast in the U.S.

Hoover Dam is located 30 miles southeast of Las Vegas on U.S. Highway 93. Tours of the dam are offered daily from 7:30 a.m. to 7:15 p.m. between Memorial Day and Labor Day and 9:00 a.m. to 4:15 p.m. during the rest of the year. There is a $1 admission charge. For more information, contact the Bureau of Reclamation, (702) 293-1081. ❧

Searchlight

Matchless Searchlight

ANYONE WHO HAS EVEN HEARD of Searchlight know it more for being the birthplace of Nevada's U.S. Senator Harry Reid than for anything else.

But Searchlight, located about an hour south of Las Vegas via U.S. Highway 95, also has the distinction of once being the largest community in southern Nevada — in fact, in 1905, it boasted nearly twice as many residents as Las Vegas.

Additionally, during the following year, Searchlight's city fathers and mothers were so convinced of the long-term prospects for the burgeoning mining community that they attempted to wrestle the county seat away from Pioche (modern day Clark County was once part of Lincoln County).

While that movement failed, the effort so encouraged the aggressive Las Vegans (who had been able to register almost as many voters as larger Searchlight) that in 1908 they were able to force the division of Lincoln County into two counties.

Ironically, historians indicate that Searchlight residents apparently didn't support this action because of concern about assuming a proportional share of the former Lincoln County's debt — which was probably why they also didn't get the seat of the newly created county.

Searchlight sprung into being in the late-1890s when gold was discovered in the area. By mid-1898, a mining district was formed and a camp began to take shape.

The town's unusual name is believed to have been derived either from a popular brand of sulphur matches (the most popular theory) or because one of the town's earliest miners remarked that you'd need a searchlight to find any valuable ore (a good second choice) or in honor of Lloyd Searchlight, owner of many claims in the area (a boring but probably accurate theory).

By 1902, the camp has a post office, a 15-mile narrow gauge railroad between the mines and a mill on the Colorado River, a newspaper, saloons and hundreds of people.

The mines continued to produce — ultimately more 40 mines which produced in excess of $7 million in ore — and by 1906, a business district had formed with dozens of shops and saloons, two newspapers, a telephone company and several mills. The town's population was estimated in 1907 to be more than 5,000 people.

Alas, as with most mining towns, the ore began to diminish the next year and the town began its long decline. Within a decade, most families had moved to more prosperous Las Vegas and only a handful of small scale mining operations continued to work the tailings. By the 1930s, the town's days as a major mining center were gone.

Today, the intrepid explorer can still find remnants of Searchlight's rich mining past — if you look beyond the obvious. At first glance, the town of several hundred seems to be little more than a wide spot in the road, although the Searchlight Nugget casino and diner still serves a 10-cent cup of coffee.

But the hillsides around Searchlight are littered with the historic refuse of an earlier day. For example, if you turn west of Highway 95 on a dirt road located about a mile north of the town, you can drive up to one of the old mining headframes.

Wandering through the high grass and sagebrush around this aging wooden giant, you can find plenty of rock foundations and wooden scraps, including the rusted, round bottoms of what must have been a row of about a half dozen old cyanide tanks.

There are also a number of open mine shafts — so be extremely careful when walking around. On a hillside to the north, you can see another headframe.

Driving into Searchlight, you can also see the large remains of another wooden headframe, an ore bin and other mining-related structures on a hill overlooking the town. A few old wooden miners shacks are sprinkled throughout the town.

The town's new community center includes a nice small museum with exhibits and displays that tell the town's mining history. The museum is open Mon.-Fri. from 9-5 and 9-12 noon on Saturdays.

If you travel 14 miles east on State Route 164, which intersects with Highway 95 in Searchlight, you can essentially retrace the old narrow gauge train route to the Cottonwood Cove recreation area on the Colorado River.

For more information, contact the Searchlight Historic Museum, Searchlight Community Center, 200 Michael Wendell Way, Searchlight, (702) 455-7955. ❧

Laughlin

Laughlin
Blooms and Booms

KEEPING UP WITH THE CHANGES in Laughlin is like trying to figure out the latest configuration of the former Soviet
Union.

During the past decade, Laughlin has virtually erupted into a
thriving resort community that nearly rivals more established
vacation destinations, like Lake Tahoe, in gaming revenues. With
more than 8,000 hotel rooms and 5,000 permanent residents,
Laughlin has become one of the state's fastest growing communities.

What makes this all the more remarkable is the fact that only
25 years ago, Laughlin, which is located about 90 miles southeast
of Las Vegas, consisted of little more than a gas station and bait
shop, with a handful of slot machines and plenty of sagebrush.

It was back then that Don Laughlin purchased land just below
Davis Dam and built the first casino and rooms in Laughlin. He
also decided the town needed a post office and approached the

proper U.S. Postal Service authorities to request permission to open one in his casino.

According to Laughlin, he suggested several names for the new community, including "Casino, Nevada," but the postal service was uncomfortable with the gaming connotations and chose his name for the town.

As recently as 1984, the town only had 95 permanent residents, mostly living in mobile homes. A drive around the community today, however, reveals several large subdivisions as well as commercial centers and office parks just south of the casino row. Additionally, the town has an 18-hole executive golf course, called "Emerald River," with plans for a municipally-owned golf course.

Like nearby Las Vegas, Laughlin has gained a reputation as a town that can make things happen, once it settles on a goal. For example, for decades, the only way to cross the Colorado River, to Bullhead City, Arizona, was via boat or by driving about 15 miles, over the top of Davis Dam.

So Don Laughlin decided to build a bridge. Naturally, he constructed this span adjacent to his property, so visitors from Arizona are literally dropped on his doorstep.

Laughlin's appeal seems to be the result of its location. It taps tourists from Phoenix , Tucson and Southern California, particularly the growing San Bernadino area. Additionally, Laughlin has carved its own niche in the gaming market. Rather than cater to the "high rollers," who traditionally favor Las Vegas and Atlantic City, Laughlin has sought the middle class gambler. Laughlin puts a premium on being comfortable and casual — you'll find no dinner jackets and evening gowns here.

Of course, there are other reasons why visitors are attracted to Laughlin. In addition to offering moderately priced meals and rooms, all of Laughlin's hotel-casinos are built either adjacent to or near the Colorado River, which provides a pleasant, relaxing contrast to the surrounding desert. A special treat is riding on the small ferries that taxi people between the hotels and parking areas on the Arizona side of the river.

Visitors can also take river cruises on the "Little Belle" paddle-wheeler or take a short tour of the nearby Davis Dam. Laughlin is located adjacent to Lake Mohave, so it offers plenty of water sports, such as fishing, houseboating and waterskiing.

While the climate can get downright hot in the summer (temperatures often climb above the 100 degree mark), winter is "Laughlintime." From December to March, while most of the country is gripped by snow and cold weather, Laughlin offers comfortable 70 to 80 degree days.

In the winter, you can frequently find parking lots filled with the recreational vehicles of "snowbirds" — RVers who live in cooler states and migrate to warmer climates in the winter months.

Despite its rapid growth, Laughlin has begun to acquire its share of new businesses and services. Several commercial airlines offer scheduled flights into the nearby Bullhead City/Laughlin Airport.

For more information, contact the Laughlin Chamber of Commerce, Box 2280, Laughlin, NV 89029, (702) 298-2214. ❧

PART II

Southern Nevada Naturally

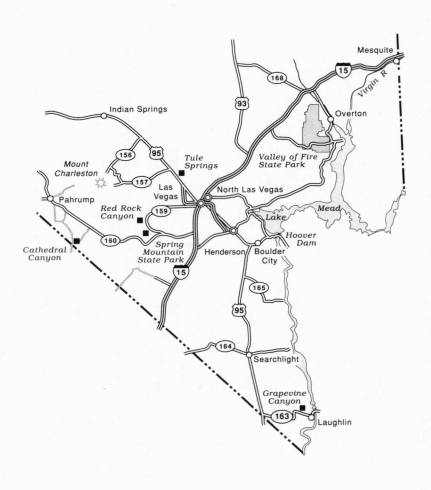

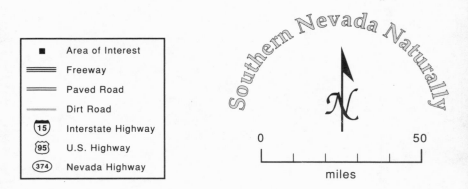

Southern Nevada Naturally

	Area of Interest
	Freeway
	Paved Road
	Dirt Road
(15)	Interstate Highway
(95)	U.S. Highway
(374)	Nevada Highway

0   50
miles

Southern Nevada Naturally

There is a rich, powerful beauty to the desert. Some look out across the Nevada landscape and see nothing but miles of emptiness. But others look at the same scene and see life, drama, history and purpose. The desert is a place of incomparable textures and colors, sensual shapes and shadows, limitless space and unfathomable mysteries. It fascinates and intimidates, presents opportunities and challenges.

As the seventh largest state, with more than 110,000 square miles, Nevada encompasses a wide variety of types of terrain, ranging from flat, sandy, dry lake beds to lush, tall, pine-covered mountains. And the southern half of the state offers just about any topography that a person could want.

In fact, it is possible, at the right time of the year, to stay in Las Vegas, drive about an hour to Mount Charleston for some downhill snow skiing in the morning, and still enjoy some water-skiing on Lake Mead in the afternoon (although that would surely make for a long, tiring day).

Out there, beyond the siren call of the slot machines and bright lights, is the natural southern Nevada. At these places, you can find green mountains to hike, unbelievable sandstone rock formations to study and a lake so large it would take an entire day to drive around.

In many ways, this is the real Nevada. It existed long before a gangster, named Bugsy, wandered out into the sagebrush, like some latter-day Brigham Young, and pronounced, "this is the place." It was old long before half-naked hunters stopped at Tule Springs to quench their thirst and roaming anasazi stopped at the mystical blood-red sandstone rocks of Valley of Fire to scratch their legacy.

Southern Nevada's natural places easily rival the more well-known landmarks, such as "Vegas Vic" and Hoover Dam. There's the Red Rock Canyon area, with its fabulous, multi-colored cliffs, the peacefulness of Spring Mountain Ranch State Park, odd and fascinating Valley of Fire and Mount Charleston, a cool, alpine refuge from the surrounding valley heat.

It all proves that Mother Nature doesn't spend all her time shooting craps at Circus Circus with Lady Luck.

Southern Nevada's Swimming Hole

CONTRARY TO THE OPINION OF SOME FOLKS, not all southern Nevada is sand, screaming neon and sagebrush. About a half hour from Las Vegas is Lake Mead, the largest man-made body of water in the Western Hemisphere.

Measuring 110 miles long, with a surface area of 274 square miles, the lake has more than 500 miles of shoreline for the thousands who daily boat, swim, waterski, hike and fish around it.

Lake Mead National Recreation Area, located 30 miles southeast of Las Vegas via U.S. Highway 93, includes the lake and surrounding area.

Like most desert lakes, Mead has a kind of incomplete feel about it. Maybe it's the lack of vegetation and trees, but there is unfinished business here — as if nature ran out of time before she could put in the landscaping.

As a result, Lake Mead has a surreal quality; something just seems amiss. There is water and there is desert — and it doesn't seem right that the two should co-exist.

Naturally, the lake benefits from this unlikely juxtaposition. The generally warm climate of the desert makes Lake Mead a mecca for sunbathing and swimming throughout the year.

Perhaps the best way to experience the lake is on one of the daily cruises offered on the Desert Princess, a Mississippi River-style paddle-wheeler, owned by the same folks who operate the M.S. Dixie paddle-wheeler on Lake Tahoe.

Lake Mead
(Photo courtesy of
Las Vegas News Bureau)

The guided hour and 15-minute journey takes you by places like the Boulder Islands, the colorful Arizona Paint Pots, Castle Reef and Sentinel Island. The boat glides up to the edge of Hoover Dam, the massive concrete slab that created Lake Mead, before returning to the marina.

It's definitely worth the price of admission.

The Lake Mead National Recreation Area includes five developed beaches and marinas with campgrounds and other services, including Overton Beach, Echo Bay, Callville Bay, the Las Vegas Wash, Temple Bar and Boulder Beach. The latter beach has a lifeguard on duty in the summer.

The Alan Bible Visitor Center near Boulder City is operated by the National Park Service, which oversees the Lake Mead area. There, you can find information about the locations of the beaches, bays and marinas as well as the intriguing plant and animal life that flourish around the lake.

Don't forget to pick up the park service's outstanding pamphlet about the lake, which includes information about fishing, swimming, boating and other activities. A map inside the brochure showing the locations of the various beaches, marinas and picnic areas.

The rangers also can tell you where you might be able to spot one of the bighorn sheep that live in the mountains around the lake as it descends to the lakeshore for a mid-day drink of water.

Fishing enthusiasts can find some excellent sport fishing at Lake Mead, including varieties like largemouth bass, rainbow trout, striped bass, channel catfish, black crappie and bluegill. You can also find plenty of some of the biggest and ugliest carp in the world clustered around the marina.

For information about the lake and recreational opportunities contact Lake Mead National Recreation Area, 601 Nevada Highway, Boulder City, NV 89005-2426, (702) 293-8907. ❧

Red Rock Canyon
(Photo courtesy of
Las Vegas News Bureau)

Colorful
Red Rock Canyon

ONE OF SOUTHERN NEVADA'S most beautiful scenic spots
is the Red Rock Canyon Recreation Area. There, visitors will find
lush natural canyons and dramatic multi-colored cliffs — all within sight of the man-made glitter of Las Vegas.

The 62,000-acre Red Rock Canyon area, located only 20 miles
from downtown Las Vegas via Charleston Boulevard, is a fascinating geologic wonderland Located on the eastern slopes of the
Spring Mountains, the region includes impressive peaks and steep
cliffs that offer excellent photography, sightseeing or hiking.

The Red Rock area is also a part of the Bureau of Land
Management's Backcountry Byway program, a series of scenic and
historic drives located throughout the west.

The unique Red Rock terrain was formed thousands of years
ago when the earth was literally turned upside down. Shifting
land masses caused the older stratas of rock (the limestone and
shale) to actually become piled atop the younger deposits of red

sandstone. Formations exposed in the area record more than 500 million years of geologic history.

Your first stop should be at the Red Rock Visitors Center. Inside, are excellent displays explaining the geology, history, plant and animal life, archeology and recreational opportunities found in the area.

A 13-mile loop road with interpretive signs starts adjacent to the Visitors Center and winds through the beautiful surroundings.

At the two mile spot on the loop road there is a paved turnout called the Calico Hills Vista. Here you can get a sweeping panoramic view of the red-pink sandstone Calico Hills that have been carefully crafted by nature and time.

About a mile farther is the turnoff to the old sandstone quarry. From a parking area, you can follow several trails that lead through a quarry, which provided sandstone blocks in the 1920s for Las Vegas home and building construction.

Trails to the east and north allow glimpses of Indian petro-glyphs (prehistoric rock writings) and mescal pits in the Brownstone Canyon. Picnic tables are also provided in the quarry area.

A few miles farther is Willow Springs, a developed picnic area with shade trees, tables, grills and restrooms. From Willow Springs, there are a number of long hiking trailes leading to the Lone Pine Springs and the Red Rock Summit.

Ahead on the loop road is another turnout, from which you can make relatively easy hikes to Ice Box and Lost Creek canyons.

You can also take an invigorating two mile day hike at nearby Pine Creek Canyon. The trail begins from the side of the loop road and continues through a wide variety of lush vegetation, including ponderosa pines, which are rare at this low elevation, and an assortment of ferns.

The presence of water and vegetation in Red Rock supports a large number of animal species. Sometimes, with binoculars and a bit of luck, you can spot bighorn sheep, bobcats, gray foxes and even wild burros at the higher elevations.

From Pine Creek, the loop road continues through equally beautiful scenery before rejoining the main road, which is Charleston Boulevard.

The Red Rock Vista is about a mile beyond the turnoff leading to Red Rock's 13-mile scenic loop road. From this overlook, you can see the picturesque layered Red Rock escarpment, a 3,000 foot high formation of red sandstone, gray limestone and shale.

From the overlook, you can also see half-hidden crevices teeming with green vegetation, including ponderosa pine trees. Many of the canyons in these mountains contain mountain streams with small waterfalls visible in the winter and spring.

For more information about the Red Rock area, contact the U.S. Bureau of Land Management, Las Vegas District, Box 7834, Las Vegas, NV 89125, (702) 388-6627 or 363-1921. ❧

Spring Mountain Ranch

Lifestyles of
The Rich and Famous

WITH ITS LUSH, GRASSY MEADOWS, spring-fed stream and acres of mature cottonwoods, sycamores and poplars, Spring Mountain Ranch State Park defies the usual image of southern Nevada.

Located just 15 miles west of Las Vegas, off West Charleston Boulevard, the ranch sits at the base of the beautiful multi-colored Wilson Cliffs, part of the spectacular Red Rock Canyon Area.

In addition to being one of the most beautiful places in southern Nevada, the ranch is also one of the most historic sites in the state. In the mid-1830s, a campsite was established alongside the creek that winds down from the nearby mountains.

The presence of clean water and grass made the location attractive to travelers journeying on one of the branches of the Spanish Trail route that passed by here. Because of its remoteness, the trail was also notorious as a hideout for local outlaws who would prey on passing pack trains.

In 1864, the site was claimed by one of the raiders, a man named Bill Williams, who apparently maintained horses there. In the mid-1870s, James Wilson and his partner, George Anderson, filed for legal ownership of the site, which they named Sand Stone Ranch.

Anderson departed in the early 1880s and Wilson assumed control of the property as well as adopted and raised Anderson's two sons. The two, Jim Wilson Jr. and Tweed, inherited the ranch after their father died in 1906.

The two operated the complex for over a decade, then sold in 1929 to a family friend, Willard George, who allowed them to live on the ranch until they died. They are buried, with their adopted father, in a small cemetery on the ranch.

George began to develop the ranch, adding a chinchilla farm (he was a Hollywood furrier by trade) as well as cattle. In 1944, George leased the ranch to actor Chester Lauck ("Lum" from the "Lum and Abner" radio show), the first of the ranch's parade of celebrity owners.

Lauck purchased the property in 1948 and began constructing the impressive New England-style cut sandstone and redwood ranch house, which today is open for tours.

Called the "Bar Nothing Ranch," Lauck used the ranch as a vacation retreat and summer camp for boys, while maintaining the cattle ranch.

In 1955, Lauck sold the now-beautifully landscaped estate to Vera Krupp, wife of the German munitions manufacturer, Alfried Krupp. She added a swimming pool and expanded both the house and the cattle operations.

Mrs. Krupp, who made the ranch her principal residence, renamed it Spring Mountain Ranch. The bucolic ranch, with its well-manicured meadows and cool shade from the southern Nevada heat, was a popular stop for the vacationing rich and famous.

The ranch was sold in 1967 to the Hughes Tool Company (later Summa Corporation) and while Howard Hughes never lived there, it was used by Summa executives.

In 1972, it was purchased by Fletcher Jones and William Murphy, two southern businessmen who planned to develop the site into a large condominium project. Public outcry resulted in the ranch being sold in 1974 to the Nevada Division of State Parks.

Today, the ranch continues to be a working cattle ranch; on a recent visit, several dozen cows were grazing on the picturesque pastures surrounding the sprawling ranch-style main house.

The setting is unexpectedly beautiful. The drive from the main road to the ranch takes you through a small forest of joshuas and yuccas, then the park seemingly erupts around you like a lush, green mirage.

The main house is open for tours Friday through Monday, 10 a.m. to 4 p.m. Additionally, guided tours of the entire 520 acres are offered on Saturdays, Sundays and holidays. This tour includes a visit to the Old Reservoir, the Wilson family cemetery, the 1880's board and batten cabin, an 1864 stone cabin and blacksmith shop and other ranch buildings.

The park's expansive picnic grounds are open daily from 8 a.m. until 7 p.m. There is a $3 day use fee. The park is also a popular location for outdoor concerts in the spring and summer months.

For more information, call the Spring Mountain Ranch at (702) 875-4141 or the Las Vegas District Office of the Nevada Division of State Parks at (702) 385-0264. ❧

Valley of Fire
(Photo courtesy of
Las Vegas News Bureau)

The Fabulous
Valley of Fire

THE LATE AFTERNOON SUN casts a strange, mutating light on the Valley of Fire's sandstone cliffs and boulders. Rocks that earlier in the day were benign oranges and browns gradually assume deeper, more dramatic shades. Angry and red.

The sun also molds the rock into new shapes. Sandstone that an hour before seemed to be nothing more than pitted rock becomes a hauntingly expressive canvas filled with long shadows, curved surfaces and hidden places.

The changes continue. A giant rock arch becomes a massive elephant. A sandstone bowl formed by rain becomes a bottomless pit and a perfect hiding place for a renegade Indian. Stone towers along the road are transformed into huge icons resembling nothing less than the colossus of Stonehenge.

At this time of day, it is easy to see why the Valley of Fire was made Nevada's first state park more than 50 years ago. The park, located on the banks of Lake Mead, is truly one of the most unique of Nevada's desert locations.

Scientists say the special sandstone qualities found in the area were formed from great shifting sand dunes found more than 150 million years ago. The region was subject to intense land movements and uplifting that helped create the present topography.

However, I prefer to believe that nature, acting like some celestial Rodin, used the wind and rain to carve the sandstone into a variety of shapes that, like quality art, is best viewed in the correct light and under the best circumstances.

The area has long held fascination for man. Fossils and other archeological evidence indicates that many prehistoric people were attracted to the valley. The earliest inhabitants included the Basketmaker people and the Anasazi Pueblo farmers from the nearly Moapa Valley (who were also the inhabitants of the famous Lost City, but that's another story).

In fact, one of the park's best attractions is the excellent collection of petroglyphs (which are prehistoric Indian rock writings) that can be found on the valley walls. A fine interpretive trail begins north of the park visitors center and leads a half-mile through the best petroglyphs in the park.

The trail ends at a place called "Mouse's Tank" because it was a favorite catchbasin for water. This particular basin was named for a renegade Indian who used the area as a hide-out and utilized the tank as one of his water supplies.

The visitors center (open daily from 8:30 a.m. to 4:30 p.m.) is a good place to begin your tour. In addition to being the only place to find a water fountain in the park, the center offers exhibits about the geology and animal life of the region, including the rare and protected desert tortoise.

The center also has good information about desert flora and fauna. Because of its location, the Valley of Fire is one of the best places in the state to watch the wildflowers bloom. In late March and early April, depending on rainfall, the park roads offer good places to spot the springtime blooms of desert marigold, indigo-bush and desert mallow.

There are plenty of places to explore in the park. Near the entrance from State Route 169, you can find the Cabins, which were native sandstone structures built in the 1930s by the Civilian Conservation Corps. The buildings are now a picnic area.

Additionally, you can view the Seven Sisters — seven huge sandstone towers that also serve as a picnic area or follow interpretive trails through a forest of petrified logs and stumps that date more than 200 million years in age. The park also has several interesting landmarks, including the Beehives, which were round sandstone formations that resemble their namesakes, and the White Domes.

At Rainbow Vista and Fire Canyon, both north of the visitor center via a paved road and a short hike, you can find two excellent sites from which to photograph the park.

The Valley of Fire also has two campgrounds (both just off the main road, west of the visitors center) with 50 campsites. The sites are equipped with shaded tables, BBQ grills, water and restrooms. There is also a recreational vehicle dump station near the campgrounds.

The Valley of Fire State Park is located about 50 miles northeast of Las Vegas. To reach it, travel south to Las Vegas on U.S. Highway 95. From Las Vegas, travel east on Interstate 15 to State Route 40. Head east for 24 miles to the park. For more information, contact the Valley of Fire State Park (702) 397-2088. ❧

Mount Charleston

Southern Nevada's Mountain Retreat

WITH ITS LUSH, PINE-COVERED CANYONS and snow-capped 11,900-foot peak, Mt. Charleston finds a way to rise above the ordinary.

Located about 50 miles north of Las Vegas, via U.S. Highway 95 and State Routes 156 and 157, Mt. Charleston is Southern Nevada's tallest point — and one of its most beautiful spots.

The peak is named after Charleston, South Carolina, home-town of several members of an Army survey team, which mapped the area in 1906. The peak is located in the majestic Spring Mountain Range, which impressively rises high over the surround-ing Las Vegas Valley.

The drive into the area is well worth the trip. After crossing nearly an hour's worth of relatively flat terrain on U.S. 95, you turn left on State Route 157 (the road to Kyle Canyon) and begin heading west.

The first thing you notice is that the surroundings quickly

begin to change as the road rises from the valley. Sagebrush and yucca plants begin to thin and, within a few miles, you reach the 5,000-foot threshold of pinyon and juniper woodlands.

This terrain continues for a few more miles, to about 6,500-feet, then gradually becomes covered with ponderosa pine and, eventually, fir and aspen. Expressive rock faces also begin to peek out from amidst the pine forests. These craggy, lined stone walls rise above the road, adding character and atmosphere to the area.

About ten miles from the highway you will reach the Mt. Charleston Hotel, a large lodge that boasts a quiet restaurant, dance floor, small casino and a huge fireplace. Constructed in 1984, the hotel has 63 rooms, with prices ranging from $50 to $130.

Farther up the road is Mt. Charleston Village, with a few residences and the U.S. Forest Service district office (most the area above 7,000 feet is supervised by the Forest Service). Nearby, at the end of the road, is the Mt. Charleston Lodge restaurant, another popular eating establishment.

From here, you can also find the starting points of several great trails including Little Falls Trail (an easy half mile trek to a small waterfall), Cathedral Rock Trail (three-quarters of a mile of moderate hiking but the best view of the area) and North Loop Trail (nine miles of more difficult terrain).

Kyle Canyon also has a dozen campsites with trailer spaces, toilets, barbecue pits and tables. You can get information about camping areas from the Forest Service office.

Back at the Mt. Charleston Hotel, you can also turn north onto Highway 158, which connects with Highway 156, the Lee Canyon Road. About three miles from the turnoff, you can find the trail to Robber's Roost, a system of limestone caverns that were once used as hideouts for local bandits.

At the top of Lee Canyon, you'll find something extremely unexpected in Southern Nevada — a nice little ski area with a base elevation of 8,500 feet. Lee Canyon offers three double-chair lifts (which take you another 1,000-feet up) and acres of quality snow providing runs of 1,000 yards to a mile long.

The ski area also has a beginner's run, a ski school and T-bar to the intermediate slope. Visitors will also find a day lounge with food and refreshments.

It's somehow appropriate that only in Las Vegas is it possible in the same day to go waterskiing at Lake Mead, then head an hour or so north to Mt. Charleston for some downhill and crosscountry skiing.

For more information about Mt. Charleston, contact the U.S. Forest Service, (702) 388-6254. ❧

Tule Springs

Tule Springs
and Early Man

TALL TULE REEDS SLOWLY WAVE in the gentle breeze. Large geese waddle down the banks of a cool spring-fed lake, then gingerly float onto the calm waters. It's easy to see why early man would have been attracted to Tule Springs.

At Tule Springs, also known as the Floyd Lamb State Park, archaeologists have discovered evidence of man having lived in the area from 11,000 to 14,000 years ago, making it one of the oldest sites of human habitation in the United States.

Floyd Lamb State Park is located 10 miles northwest of Las Vegas, via U.S. Highway 95 and Durango Drive. The park is clearly marked from the highway.

In 1933, an archaeologist discovered bones of animals and humans that, following carbon dating, indicated man had used the watering hole more than 10,000 years ago.

The discovery was considered important because it was the first proof of the existence of man in Pleistocene times, thousands of years earlier than previously believed. Indeed, it appears that the area once consisted of several springs and was covered with sagebrush and bordered with yellow pine forests.

Additionally, the evidence indicated that those early inhabitants were more advanced than scientists had thought. Scientists have uncovered prehistoric hearths, fluted arrows, spear points, scrapers and charred animal bones.

Because of the presence of water, the area was a center of activity for big game animals and humans, who apparently hunted the animals. Fossils found there have included extinct prehistoric ground sloths, mammoths, horses and camels as well as the giant condor.

The springs continued to be essential to the development of the west. Later evidence showed the region was populated by small groups of Desert Culture people, about 7,000 years ago, who survived on native vegetation and small game.

A horse-changing station developed at the springs in the early 20th century, servicing horse-drawn wagon and freight trains traveling between the mining camps to the north and the railroad station at Las Vegas.

Later, the area became a dude ranch, of the type popular during the state's "divorce capital" era in the 1920s and 30s. Many of the original whitewash and green-trimmed ranch buildings can still be found on the site.

The park, created about a decade ago, is named for a controversial former state Senator who was one of the longest serving members of the Legislature.

It encompasses about 700 acres, which include nature trails, picnic tables, gazebos and lakes for fishing. Within the park, there is also a state arboretum and nursery.

Standing beside the large spring-fed lake in the center of the park, it's easy to appreciate how important the site must have been to Nevada's earliest inhabitants. The area is literally an oasis in the desert with its green lawns, lush tule reeds and mature trees.

Adjacent to the park, the Las Vegas Gun Club operates a popular shooting range (which is a little incongruous next to the park) as well as provides parking for recreational vehicles.

There is a $3 day use fee for the park, which is open during daylight hours (no camping is allowed). For more information, contact the Nevada Division of State Parks, 687-4384. ❧

Refreshing
The Senses

AN UNCANNY THING ABOUT THE DESERT is that — despite obvious appearances — it finds a way to support and sustain life.

A good example is Grapevine Canyon, located about eight miles northwest of Laughlin, which is as close to a natural sanctuary as you'll find in this desolate part of southern Nevada.

To reach Grapevine Canyon, head west from Laughlin on State Route 163 for about six miles. Turn right on a marked dirt road (there is a Bureau of Land Management sign there) and follow the signs for two miles to the canyon.

The road to the canyon ends at a trailhead, where you can park your car or truck (motorized vehicles are prohibited from this point) From here, you must hoof it about a half mile on a flat trail to the mouth of the canyon.

The trail runs parallel to a wall of expressive sandstone rocks, about an eighth of a mile on the left, as well as a dry creek bed on the right. The rocks have been pocked and shaped into interesting shapes, a few of which bear a remarkable resemblance to contemporary impressionist sculptures.

Along the way, you pass through thick sagebrush, a few joshua trees, mesquite bushes and, closer to the rocks, a handful of beautiful barrel cactus plants. On the day I was visiting, there was also the strong, rich fragrance of sagebrush in the air.

The trail reaches a narrow passage in the rocks and it is here that you finally begin to experience the true beauty and fascination of Grapevine Canyon.

A small stream of water pours through the canyon opening and spills into the creek bed, where it evaporates a few hundred yards beyond. And just ahead, you can hear the unmistakable sounds of a gurgling creek, its precious water splashing down and over several rock ledges — like a small series of waterfalls.

Additionally, carved into the surrounding rock are dozens of ancient petroglyphs, some appearing to almost have been drawn on top of each other. The images include geometric patterns (rounded and square shapes) as well as small drawings of bighorn sheep and stick figures apparently representing humans.

The setting provides a clue as to why such a great number of petroglyphs are to be found here. Hunters would hide in these rocks patiently awaiting deer, sheep and other game that would be attracted to the canyon by the presence of fresh water.

Naturally, the wait might be considerable, and one can imagine these people carving various symbols — perhaps, for good luck — into the sandstone while waiting for dinner to wander along.

The trail passes through the canyon mouth and the wall of petroglyphs (and there are quite a few), then heads up into the canyon. Here, you can find a fairly healthy stream of water (with small pools filled with pollywogs) tumbling down the rocks as well as a thick patch of namesake wild grapevines.

The main dirt road, from which you turned west to reach Grapevine Canyon, is also the route to Christmas Tree Pass, another noteworthy scenic trip. From Grapevine Canyon, it is about seven miles along the backside of the Newberry Mountains to the 3,500 foot pass. The dirt road eventually connects with U.S. Highway 95, just south of Cal Nev Ari.

For more information, contact the Superintendent, Lake Mead National Recreation Area, 601 Nevada Highway, Boulder City, NV 89005-2426, (702) 293-8907. 🍂

Grapevine Canyon

PART III

East Side Stories

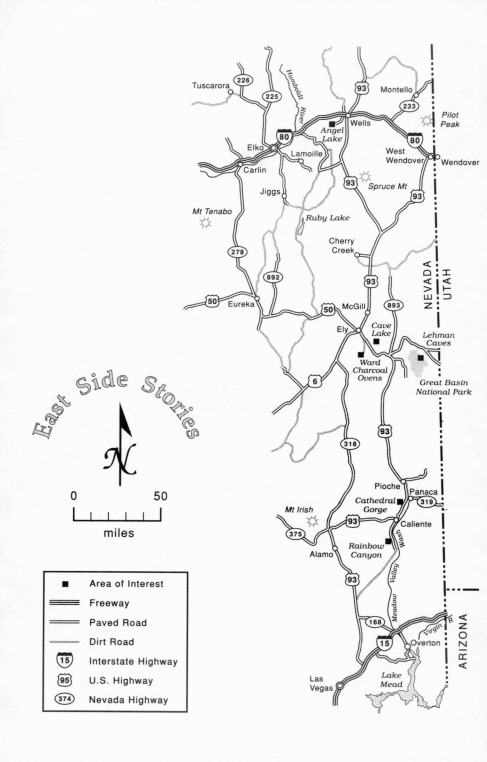

East Side
Stories

Traveling through the eastern side of Nevada reminds me of that old axiom: if a tree fell in a forest, but there was no one to hear it, would it make any noise? Suppose you put the most magnificent scenery in Nevada on the eastern side but no one came to see it, would it still be beautiful? You bet.

Eastern Nevada is truly God's Country. Despite its sparse population, it contains the largest concentration of state parks — four in Lincoln County alone — which highlight some of the most picturesque, unique countryside found in the state.

It's easy to drive Highway 93, which is eastern Nevada's lifeline (also the state's only official scenic highway), and imagine how the earliest pioneers must have seen the state. Unbelievably long, wide valleys, majestic mountain ranges and unusual geology — all virtually untouched — are just a few of the reasons this is such a wonderful part of the state to explore.

The east side of the state includes places like the Lost City Museum in Overton, a repository of artifacts and information about the state's earliest residents, the Anasazi. North is Rainbow Canyon and the Meadow Valley Wash, containing a number of scenic and historic places, including some of the best petroglyphs in Nevada.

Caliente is the railtown that has refused to relinquish its last links with the railroad from which it was spawned, while nearby Cathedral Gorge State Park is a fascinating study on the impacts of erosion over a few centuries. The town of Pioche is a mining historian's dream come true as is the ghost camp of Cherry Creek, north of Ely.

And, of course, there are the quiet, postcard-pretty fishing holes, Angel and Cave lakes, as well as booming Wendover, the town that proves anything can grow and thrive in the desert with enough care and feeding. Along the way, you pass through more than a half dozen magnificent mountain ranges, with names like Snake, Schell Creek, East Humboldt, Egan, Cherry Creek, Hiko and Pahranagat.

My favorite time out here is in the early evening, when the western sun finally begins to settle down somewhere beyond California and the mountains are bathed in a soft red-purple hue. For that short period of time — usually no more than fifteen minutes or so — the mountains, the sky and the valleys become truly mysterious; the shadow and light share secrets, while the wind whispers tales behind your back.

Eastern Nevada is rugged, larger-than-life, Edna Ferber country where a man or woman's measure is gauged not by the size of a paycheck or whether you wear the right kind of designer jeans, but by how hard you can work and whether your word means anything.

A colleague of mine once described folks who live out in those seemingly remote, small rural Nevada towns — such as those you'll find along the state's east side — as "fiercely proud."

He's right. ❧

Finding
The Lost City

LONG BEFORE OGDEN, FREMONT OR CARSON set foot in Nevada, the land was home to the "Anasazi" or "Ancient Ones," native people who developed a major civilization that stretched the length of a valley bordered by Warm Springs and the Virgin River in southern Nevada.

History indicates that the Anasazi mysteriously disappeared — some speculate they were driven from the valley because of drought, famine or disease — about 800 years ago, probably migrating to the areas that became Arizona and New Mexico.

Today, the best place to learn about Nevada's prehistoric Native American culture is at the Lost City Museum in Overton at the north end of Lake Mead. The museum contains one of the largest and most complete collections of early Pueblo Indian artifacts in the southwest.

The museum is located on one of the Anasazi village sites. On the grounds, you can find several Pueblo-type structures, made of wattle and daub, that have been reconstructed on the original foundations.

Inside, you'll be treated to hundreds of rare arrowheads, baskets, atlatl (or throwing spears), skins and pottery. Additionally, one wing of the museum includes a re-creation of an ancient Pueblo Indian village site.

The Anasazi's village is also called "Pueblo Grande de Nevada," because of its size, or the Lost City, because no one knows why it was abandoned.

Many of the artifacts in the museum were collected during excavations of the area in the late 1930s, during the time that Lake Mead was filling up with the waters held by Hoover Dam. Since then, additional excavations on the banks of the lake have continued to yield new information about these important people.

The Lost City has provided valuable information about the Anasazi's transition from a nomadic desert tribe, before the time of Christ, to a more sophisticated society that built permanent settlements and planted crops.

Displays in the museum illustrate the history of the Anasazis. For instance, the earliest residents, called the "Basketmakers," generally lived in open areas or natural shelters and created fine woven baskets from the local willows and yucca plants. Their diet consisted of plants and hunted game, like deer and rabbits, brought down with the use of an atlatl.

Later, in a time called the Late Basketmaker period, the people adopted the ways of surrounding cultures and begin using a bow and arrow, planting crops and building pithouses in the valley.

That was followed by the Pueblo period, during which the people began living in above-ground buildings with underground storage units. It was during this time, that the Indians began producing painted pottery and developed a social structure, religious practices, trade and crude writing.

Fine examples of petroglyphs — or Indian rock writing — can

90

be found carved into rocks throughout the Lost City area. In 1150 A.D., the Puebloans mysteriously departed and the area eventually became home for the early Paiutes, whose descendents still remain in the state.

In addition to displays about the Anasazi, the museum also contains exhibits detailing the earliest white settlers in the area, starting with Mormon farmers, who began cultivating the area in the 1860s.

The Lost City Museum is located on State Route 169 in the small farming community of Overton, about 60 miles northeast of Las Vegas. The museum is open daily from 8:30 a.m. to 4:30 p.m. For more information, call 397-2193. ❧

Lost City Museum

Meadow Valley Wash

Magnificent
Meadow Valley Wash

PART ONE

NEVADA'S GEOLOGIC HISTORY is a crazy-quilt of upheavels, eruptions, faulting and just about anything else that can be done to a place — and one of the best ways to see it is on the backroads of eastern Nevada.

Eastern Nevada is a geologist's dream with its expressive, multi-colored rock canyon cliffs and massive, layered stone formations that poke through the earth's surface at seemingly random angles.

Because the region is fairly remote, it's also still possible to travel these dirt and gravel backroads and see stone formations untouched or influenced by the effects of man.

Perhaps the best of these many off-the-beaten-pathways in Nevada is the Meadow Valley Wash road leading from Glendale (which is 45 miles east of Las Vegas on Interstate 15) to the historic eastern Nevada railroad community of Caliente.

The road, which is only accessible with a four-wheel drive

vehicle, travels some 75 miles over somewhat rugged dirt roads. The road, located about 2 miles north of Glendale, just off State Route 168, runs parallel to the Union Pacific Railroad tracks for much of the way (be careful to watch for occasional trains since you're literally driving beside the tracks).

The trip begins slowly as you pass through typical high desert sage and grass country. Within a few miles you can see, to the right, some beautiful eroded plateaus, which are part of the Mormon Mountains. These deep, naturally-carved mounds, just off in the distance, are the kind of panoramic vistas that seem to be found only in eastern Nevada.

Driving along, the ground changes to a more reddish color, reflecting the rich clay content in the soil. At about the 15-mile point, the road enters a different terrain, of canyons and mountainsides.

Here, you view some impressive red and brown cliff faces, along with others that are deeply carved, like the lined, weather-beaten face of a wise, old rancher.

At about the 24-mile point, the road reaches a yucca-filled canyon lined with crumbled stone cliffs, the surfaces of which are layered like a giant stack of pancakes. Illustrating the tremendous forces that have shaped this land, the layers generally run in a horizontal direction but in uneven lines due to the earth's past movements.

Stopping for a moment to admire the scenery, one can't help but be humbled by the immense power of the earth, which can thrust, crack or drop these layered rock sheets upward, then twist them and, sometimes, overturn them.

As the road continues to wind through these various canyons and passages, you also wonder how the railroad's designers came upon this route and the incredible effort it must have required to build it.

Some of the concrete railroad bridges show dates ranging from

1921 to the 1940s (and a few newer steel spans without dates), indicating this rail line is a living thing, continually requiring upkeep, replacement and care. To accent this point, it's not uncommon to stumble upon a road crew doing some kind of work on the railroad or adjacent road.

These bridges cross several marshy areas and small creeks and reinforce the fact that the road runs down the middle of Meadow Valley Wash, a natural plain that has, on occasion, been subject to intense flashfloods. Historic records indicate the track has been washed away several times.

At about 35 miles from the start, the road branches away from the tracks and runs parallel, but at some distance. Modest ranches with cultivated fields, horses and cows begin to appear as the terrain flattens out into a wider valley. You can also drive faster now, racing along at 35 miles per hour rather than the previous crawl speeds of 15 to 20 m.p.h.

Following another 20 miles of fairly smooth driving, you reach Elgin, which is nothing more than a name on the map. A little farther is the Bradshaws' End of the Rainbow Ranch, a small, local resort with a small fishing pond and picnic areas. It is open in the summer.

The ranch, established in the 1880s, offers wonderful apples (Jonathan or Delicious varieties) in the fall and boasts that it has the only naturally-watered apple orchards in the state.

From here, you enter the Rainbow Canyon area.

For specific information about driving the Meadow Valley Wash road, consult the Nevada Map Atlas produced by the Nevada Department of Transportation. This spiral-bound book, which sells for $12, is an invaluable resource for traveling the state's backroads. Contact NDOT, 1263 Stewart St., Carson City, NV 89710, (702) 687-5585. ✒

Rainbow Canyon

Colorful
Rainbow Canyon

PART TWO

THE SECOND HALF OF OUR JOURNEY through Eastern Nevada's magnificent Meadow Valley Wash country begins at the southern entrance to the scenic and historic Rainbow Canyon, about 20 miles south of Caliente.

So named because of the range of colors found in the rocks of the tall walls lining this long, narrow natural depression, Rainbow Canyon was created by intense volcanic activity more than 34 million years ago.

Geologists say that over a period of many millions of years, layers of ash deposits — caused by volcanoes that were active in this time — began to settle, then form into rock called "tuff."

Later, these layers began to crack and hot water, laden with additional minerals, flowed into these fault areas, depositing gold, iron, copper, manganese and a number of other materials within the fractures.

Rainbow Canyon's broad canvas of colors was created when these mineral deposits stained the tuffs. Iron ores created the red and yellow shades, while copper caused the blue and green hues. The white cliffs are the remains of pure deposits of the volcanic ash.

About a million years ago, a volcanic chamber, under much of what is now eastern Nevada, collapsed, creating a large valley that eventually filled with water. Faulting at the southern end of this lake valley later allowed the water to escape and, ultimately, carved the area now called Rainbow Canyon.

The presence of water in Rainbow Canyon (a creek continues to run down the middle of the canyon) also helped attract Nevada's earliest residents. Artifacts found in the area indicate the presence of man some 3,500 years ago in Rainbow Canyon.

Fortunately for us, there are still plenty of places where we can still find evidence of both the geologic and prehistoric roots of the canyon. The latter are best represented by the large number of petroglyphs — prehistoric rock carvings — found in the area.

Some of the best of these rock writings can be found about 17.3 miles south of Caliente. On the slopes of the west side of the canyon are a handful of boulders that have been carved with a variety of symbols and designs, including some remarkable big horn sheep drawings.

Farther down the road, on the east side (about 18 miles south of Caliente), are additional drawings depicting circular shapes, squiggles and other intriguing designs. Local folks indicate there are dozens of similar sites throughout the canyon.

The drawings are believed to be the work of the "Anasazi" or ancient ones, prehistoric people who resided in the American southwest. The meaning of these carved shapes remains unknown, although many believe they have religious significance related to the harvest and hunt.

In addition to petroglyphs, investigators have found other artifacts from these original residents, including arrow heads, baskets, sandal fragments and grinding tools.

At a place called Etna Cave (in a canyon about 5 miles south of Caliente on the west side of the canyon), you can also find pictographs, which are painted figures on the rock faces. Here, the red-orange drawings depict stick figures and geometric shapes.

The geologic history of the area is equally fascinating. At almost any place along the road, you will find the beautiful multi-colored, layered cliff faces that make the canyon so remarkable.

A particularly impressive formation is the sheer rock cliffs located about 15 miles south of Caliente. Here, you can find steep, gray cliffs that touch the road. Locals note that a mountain climber from Las Vegas frequently practices on the cliffs in the summer.

Also, to the east of the main road near the 15 miles point, is a dirt road leading to the entrance of Grapevine Canyon. From here, you have to hike into the canyon, which offers equally scenic cliff formations and more petroglyphs and pictographs.

Only two miles from Caliente is the site of the former (and hopefully future) Kershaw-Ryan State Park. This small park, which has been called the most beautiful in the state park system, has officially been closed since facilities and roadways were destroyed about seven years ago by severe flooding. Plans call for rebuilding Kershaw-Ryan.

Mormon pioneers discovered Rainbow Canyon in the 1870s and 1880s. Within a few years, a handful of ranches cropped up in the area to provide produce and livestock for the booming silver camps at Pioche.

In the early part of this century, the canyon was the site of an unusual competition between two rival railroad companies, the Union Pacific and the San Pedro, Los Angeles and Salt Lake Railroad. At one point, the two rail companies were building parallel grades on either sides of the canyon in a race to be the first to complete a line from Los Angeles to Salt Lake City.

Eventually, the two companies agreed to joint ownership and a single line was constructed. Since then, the track has been moved several times following major floods as the railroad has sought to find the safest route.

An excellent brochure describing the geology and history of Rainbow Canyon is available from the Caliente Chamber of Commerce, Box 255, Caliente, NV 89008, (702) 726-3129. ❧

Caliente Depot

Lincoln County's
Hot Spot

THE FIRST THING ANYONE NOTICES about Caliente is the depot. It's not one of those tiny one-room generic yellow and brown wooden railroad depots. No, Caliente's Depot is something quite special — two-stories tall and constructed of tan stucco using a classic Mission-style architecture.

It's obvious that once upon a time some visionary saw this small eastern Nevada town in a different light. The depot, which overwhelms its surroundings, seems big enough to accommodate Las Vegas or Reno.

Not surprisingly, the depot is the focal point for the community. It is the town symbol and to a large extent the whole reason for Caliente's existence. Caliente was created in 1901 when construction began on a new railroad line linking Salt Lake City to Los Angeles.

There was a right-of-way dispute, which was finally resolved when rancher Charles Culverwell, who owned the land where

Caliente is now located, allowed one railroad grade to be built through his land. Ultimately, the two factions reconciled and the Union Pacific Railroad assumed control of the project.

The railroad line was completed in 1905 and Caliente was designated a division point. Two years later, a spur was built connecting Caliente with the then-productive mines in nearby Pioche.

The impressive depot was constructed in 1923. Originally, the first floor included the railroad station, private offices and a community center, while the second level was a hotel.

Within a few years, Caliente grew to more than 5,000 residents. Some civic boosters believed the town would grow even larger because, in addition to being an important railroad stop, the town had natural hot springs. They hoped to exploit these waters, which are the source of the town's name ("caliente" is Spanish for "hot").

Alas, this future never quite came to pass, although several commercial hot springs have operated in the area over the years.

A visit today offers a rare opportunity to see a true company town in Nevada that hasn't changed too much over the years. Best example of this fact is the neat row of nearly-identical homes, built by the railroad, which are adjacent to the tracks on the northeast end of town.

The town's main commercial district also reflects the influence of the railroad as many stores and other businesses are oriented toward the tracks rather than along the highway.

The depot remains in use as a railroad station (although the train only stops once a day — practically in the middle of the night) as well as city offices, the town library and as the county commission chambers.

At the south end of the depot building is a small display of historic railroad depot equipment, such as an old freight cart, as well as information about the town. For instance, did you know that Caliente is also known as the "Rose City," and even entered a rose-covered float in the Rose Bowl Parade many decades ago.

The famed hot springs are also still around. Visitors can soak in modest private baths in the appropriately named Caliente Hot Spring Motel, on the north end of town.

In addition to its own rich history, Caliente also happens to sit in the middle of some of the most beautiful country in the state. To the south is magnificent Rainbow Canyon and, within 50 miles of the town, are no less than four state parks, including Beaver Dam, Cathedral Gorge, Spring Valley and Echo Canyon.

Caliente is located about three and a half hours north of Las Vegas via U.S. Highway 93. For more information, contact the Caliente Chamber of Commerce, (702) 726-3129. ~

Cathedral Gorge
(Photo courtesy of
Nevada Division of State Parks)

Incredible
Cathedral Gorge

THERE ARE PLENTY OF UNUSUAL PLACES in the state, but one of the strangest and most otherworldly has to be Cathedral Gorge State Park, located in Eastern Nevada.

It's hard to imagine you haven't somehow been suddenly carried off to another planet — or at least to some other dimension — when you visit this unique natural scenic wonder.

Cathedral Gorge State Park is located in the heart of Lincoln County, about 165 miles north of Las Vegas via U.S. Highway 93 on the eastern side of the state.

Tall, deeply-grooved, red-brown clay spires rise high above a narrow valley. Deep, shadowy crevices peek out from the surrounding craggy cliffs, hinting at hidden places and dark passageways leading into the unknown.

Cathedral Gorge is a place of great texture and beauty. Standing before the gorge's expressive formations and shapes, you can't help but be reminded of the fact that Nevada contains an amazing variety of types of terrain and landscape — and you've found another example.

The drive into the gorge doesn't really prepare you for what you'll find. After turning off from the highway, you enter a small valley. Along the north side (take the road to the right, the left goes to the campgrounds) you begin to notice the dusty, tan clay walls that have been carved by erosion.

A bit farther, the walls become taller and more deeply-lined; as if wizened by all that this gorge has seen and heard over the past million years. Then, quickly, you find yourself overwhelmed by immense stone walls and formations, each more unusual and fascinating than its neighbor.

Cathedral Gorge's development can be traced to more than a million years ago, when much of eastern Nevada was under water. Apparently, several streams once drained into a lake that covered much of this valley. In addition to water, these streams carried tons of silt and clay into the valley, eventually depositing hundreds of feet of sediment.

When the lake dried up, the clay deposits became exposed to the wind, sun and rain. During the past several hundred thousand years, this bentonite clay lake bed was carved and shaped by the elements into the marvelous place now called Cathedral Gorge.

The area gained its name around the turn of the century by local folks who thought the gothicly-inspired clay walls and formations resembled a church's spires. The area was designated a state park in 1935, making it one of the oldest in the state park system.

The gorge contains a number of interesting hikes, which are marked for visitors. Two lead from a parking area, at the end of the paved road, to the Moon and Canyon caves, which are actually narrow passages that wind through the dramatic clay walls.

Additionally, along the way, you may notice a couple of man-made structures, including an old stone water tower and the wooden overhangs at a picnic area in the gorge, that were constructed in the 1930s.

Also at the end of the paved road, a longer, one-mile trail leads up into the center of the gorge and affords the most impressive scenery. Way back there, deep in the clay, far from the parking area and picnic tables, you can truly feel like you've gone where no one has gone before.

At the end of the trail is a set of wooden stairs that lead up to an alternate entrance to the gorge, Miller's Point Overlook. At this end, you can look out over the entire valley, admiring nature's magnificent clay sculptures from above.

You can drive to Miller's Point Overlook by continuing north on Highway 93 to about a mile beyond the Cathedral Gorge main entrance. The overlook also offers four covered picnic tables and pit toilets.

In addition to the gorge's gorgeous (I tried to resist the pun as long as I could) scenery, the park also offers 16 campsites with toilets and showers (the water runs from mid-April to mid-November). There is a $5 park use fee.

For more information, contact the Nevada Division of State Parks, (702) 687-4384. ❧

Million Dollar Courthouse, Pioche

Rough, Tough
Pioche

THERE'S A STORY THEY LIKE TO TELL in Pioche that nearly 75 men were buried in the cemetery there before anyone died of natural causes.

Even if the story isn't true, there is little doubt that Pioche was a tough little town in its early years. According to some reports, from 1871-1872, nearly 60 percent of Nevada's killings occurred in Pioche.

Silver was discovered in Pioche in 1863 by a Mormon missionary who was shown some ore by members of the local Paiute tribe. In 1868, San Francisco financier Francois Pioche purchased claims and paid for construction of a smelter in the area.

A mining camp formed around the activity, which eventually became the community of Pioche. While the town was named after its financial benefactor, ironically he never set foot there.

By 1871, Pioche had 7,000 residents, including a rather flourishing saloon industry. To accommodate its equally rapid-growing criminal element, that was also the year the town began construction of its most famous public building — the "Million Dollar Courthouse."

The county contracted to build the courthouse at a cost of $26,400. By the time it was completed a year later, costs had escalated to more than $88,000 because of cost overruns, mismanagement and kickbacks.

Unable to pay the building bonds because of a mining slump and corrupt officials, the county refinanced the building several times over subsequent decades, each time adding interest. By the 1880s, the debt had risen to $181,000, and by the end of the century it was more than $670,000.

By the time the courthouse debt was finally retired in 1937 — four years after the building had been condemned — the total cost was nearly $1 million, hence the famous moniker.

Today, visitors can tour the restored courthouse (restoration costs were considerably less than the original cost), which is a fine local museum. The building is also used for community meetings and occasional theatrical performances.

Located about four hours northeast of Las Vegas via U.S. Highway 93, Pioche remains a quiet, friendly community that has retained much of the flavor of its early days.

Many of the buildings on its main street are authentic frontier structures with white balconies and western-style false storefronts. A few of the buildings, such as the Odd Fellows Hall, have been restored.

In the center of town is the Lincoln County Historical Museum. Inside, visitors will find artifacts from the region's frontier years, including a nice collection of antique photos, organs and clothing.

A special treat at the museum is that, for a few dollars, you can purchase an actual turn-of-the-century mining certificate (for the "Pioche Last Chance Mine"). Apparently, the museum found a whole pad of these early 20th century certificates and sells them to raise money for operations.

Also on the main street is a fine art gallery named after Francois Pioche. Inside is a variety of interesting paintings, including water colors of street scenes and area landscapes completed by a local artist in the 1870s. The paintings were found in an attic after having been lost for more than a century.

Another intriguing landmark in Pioche is an aerial tram system that runs over the mountain that overlooks the town. Constructed during a short mining boom in the 1930s — Pioche has had several false restarts over the years — the tram carried ore from mines on the hillsides south of town to the Godbe Mill and Smelter, located just north of the community.

If you climb to the top of the hill overlooking the town, you can get a closer view of the tram, which still has ore carts suspended from its thick, rusted steel cable. Additionally, you will find an outstanding overview of the area.

While exploring, however, keep in mind that there are abandoned, open mine shafts all over the surrounding hillsides. Be careful not to enter any of these old mines because they are not safe.

Pioche is located about four hours northeast of Las Vegas via U.S. Highway 93. For more information, contact the Pioche Chamber of Commerce, P.O. Box 127, Pioche, NV 89403, Hours: 11 a.m. - 3 p.m. weekdays, or call (702) 962-5544. ❧

Cave Lake

Cave Lake
and the
Ward Charcoal Ovens

W HILE THE GREAT BASIN NATIONAL PARK gets much of the ink when it comes to writing about scenic and historic sites in eastern Nevada, there are other equally fascinating places to visit in the area, such as Cave Lake and the Ward Charcoal Ovens.

The Cave Lake State Recreation Area, located about 15 miles southeast of Ely, just off Highway 93, offers the combination of impressive mountain scenery, great camping and some of the best fishing in the state.

The marked, paved road to the lake, called Success Loop Road, offers a hint of what is to come. As you rise above the sagebrush carpet, you notice expressive limestone formations that stand like elegant guardians at the entrance to the lake.

The road passes through a narrow canyon that leads to the lake, which is actually a 32-acre manmade reservoir (there's a small dam at the north end).

The dark emerald lake is situated in a scenic niche in the mountains, surrounded by forests of pinyon and juniper. Above the lake is a small yawning cave — the namesake of the lake — and ridges of rough, crumbling granite peaks weathered by countless centuries of icy winters and hot summers.

The recreation area offers a variety of activities with 20 developed campsites, showers, restrooms, a dump station, picnic areas and a dock for small fishing boats.

The lake is extremely popular for fishing and regularly stocked with brown and rainbow trout — the locals point out that the state record brown trout was caught in the lake a few years ago.

A five-mile hiking trail begins near the entrance to the recreation area and affords a pleasant opportunity to wander through the trees, enjoying the beautiful scenery and peaceful surroundings.

For those wanting a more backcountry experience, Success Loop Road continues above the lake, deeper into the mountain range. While unpaved beyond this point, it is a maintained gravel road accessible to most cars.

Adjacent to the road in this beautiful back country, you will find plenty of undeveloped but usable campsites, some hidden in small groves of white-barked quaking aspen and parallel to a small stream.

Above the road is genuinely breathtaking mountain scenery, including carved, bowl-shaped peaks that look like glacial cirques. As you admire the view, you can't help but think that someday, the area should be part of some kind of park or wilderness area.

Success Loop continues for about another 30 miles, with the best part being the first ten miles or so. If you follow it all the way, the road winds through the mountains and a few small valleys before dropping back to U.S. Highway 93 near the tiny community of McGill.

A few miles from the entrance to Cave Lake is the road leading to the Ward Charcoal Ovens, a state historical site. These massive beehive-shaped stone structures were built in 1876, when a mining district was created in the nearby community of Ward.

The ovens, which each stand 30-feet high and 25-feet wide at the base, were used to process 35 cords of wood at a time. The wood was turned into charcoal for the nearby smelters.

To reach Cave Lake, head south of Ely on Highway 93 for about eight miles. Turn right on Success Loop Road and continue for seven miles to the recreation area. Cave Lake is located in the Schell Creek Range, an impressive wall of rock directly east of Ely.

The Ward Charcoal Ovens are located about seven miles from Highway 93 via a maintained dirt road (there's an historic marker noting the spot). Three miles south of the charcoal ovens are the few remains of the town of Ward, an old mining camp.

For more information about Cave Lake or the Ward Charcoal Ovens, contact the Nevada Division of State Parks, P.O. Box 761, Ely, NV 89301, (702) 728-4467. &

McGill

The Consummate
Company Town

NEVADA HAS A NUMBER OF "company towns," most of which, not surprisingly, were created by some kind of mining business. One of the best preserved — and longest lived — is the former mining town of McGill in eastern Nevada.

Located 12 miles north of Ely via U.S. Highway 93, McGill is a classic example of a company town. Practically everyone here worked on the "smelter" (originally the Steptoe Valley Mining & Smelter Company and later, the Kennecott Copper Corporation).

Founded in 1906, McGill was originally a tent city that rose in the flats near where the Steptoe Valley Mining Company built a massive smelter. The smelter was used to melt down the copper ore mined in the Ruth area and extract the metal.

Within a year, however, more substantial concrete homes were erected for the mining company officials and a small business district began to take shape. To provide housing for workers, the company also began building modest wooden homes for them —

hence the nearly-identical, "cookie-cutter" appearance of many of the small, older houses still found in McGill.

In 1908, the Nevada Northern Railway was extended through McGill, where a depot was sited, on its journey to Cobre, a transfer point on the Southern Pacific Railroad, located about 130 miles north of Ely.

By the 1920s, McGill had grown to rival nearby Ely as the largest town in White Pine County. Even a disasterous fire in 1922, which destroyed a large part of the smelting complex, didn't slow McGill's progress, which peaked in 1930, with more 3,000 residents in the company town.

The unusually long life of the Ruth/Ely area's copper mines also contributed to McGill's longevity. For much of the next fifty years, McGill maintained a relatively steady population of about 2,000 people, most working for the smelter.

During its more than 70-year ride on the copper mining crest, McGill also acquired many of the trappings of a community, including several churches, a newspaper, a movie theater, a large brick schoolhouse and a municipal swimming pool — which was actually a large hole in the ground surrounded by trees.

Additionally, as a result of the mining company's aggressive recruiting of new immigrants to America, (including signing up people right off the boat at Ellis Island in New York) McGill became one of Nevada's most ethnically-diverse communities.

Large numbers of Greeks, Slavs and other newcomers to the promised land of America — including my Irish grandfather and uncle — found themselves in McGill working in the smelter.

But, as with all mining towns, when the mines shut down, most of the jobs disappeared. In this case, McGill's day of reckoning arrived in the early 1980s when Kennecott closed its eastern Nevada operations, including the venerable smelter.

Much of the town's population began to drift away during the 1980s — I can remember that you could buy one of those quaint, old two bedroom miner's homes for about $10,000 in the mid-80s.

Construction of a maximum security state prison in the late 1980s, however, once again brought people to McGill.

Today, while McGill hasn't completely recovered from the loss of Kennecott, it's certainly in better shape than a few years ago. Many of the identical "company" homes have been repainted and fixed up by the new residents.

The downtown business district, however, remains a mix of merchants who have survived and shuttered buildings, including a fully-stocked drug store that the owners just locked up and walked away from about ten years ago.

Unfortunately, Kennecott has removed nearly all of the historic remains of the smelter, except for the huge concrete smoke stack, which can still be seen from miles away. The former site is now a graded field.

Perhaps the most unique place in the former mining town is the McGill Club, a local bar and social club. With its 100-plus-year-old backbar and smoky ambiance, the McGill Club is a throwback to the days when neighborhood saloons had personality and character (and no ferns).

In fact, veteran Nevada travel writer David Toll once called it one of the two best bars in the state (the equally eccentric Joe's Tavern in Hawthorne being the other).

A particularly touching aspect of the McGill Club is the wall near the entrance which contains dozens of old, yellowed black and white photographs of clean-cut young men. The wall commemorates local men who have over the years served in the military and, in some cases, lost their lives in various wars.

To learn more about McGill, contact the White Pine Chamber of Commerce, 636 Aultman, Ely, NV 89301, (702) 289-8877. ᨶ

Cherry Creek

Cherry Creek
Beats the Odds

OVER THE YEARS, it has lost its railroad, its mining industry and most of its people, yet the historic eastern Nevada mining town of Cherry Creek has somehow managed to survive into the 20th century.

Cherry Creek is located 53 miles north of Ely (which sits about 300 miles east of Carson City via U.S. Highway 50). To reach the town, travel 45 miles north of Ely on U.S. Highway 93, then head west for eight miles on State Route 489.

The community of Cherry Creek has a long and colorful history. Gold and silver were found near the town in 1872. Within a few months, more than 1,000 people had moved into the boomtown and, by the middle of the following year, the town had a post office, a Wells Fargo office, several saloons and a number of other businesses.

Between 1872 and 1883, the town generally thrived as the mines continued to produce quality gold and silver ore. By the late 1870s, several large stamp mills were operating in the area to accommodate the local mines.

In 1881, additional discoveries caused several businesses from other eastern Nevada mining camps to relocate to Cherry Creek, including the White Pine News, a newspaper formerly in Hamilton.

A year later, Cherry Creek made an unsuccessful attempt to wrestle the county seat from the mining camp of Hamilton, which was in decline.

Unfortunately, Cherry Creek's mines were beginning to wane. Less valuable ore was being extracted and, unlike the town's previous slumps, no new, major discoveries were made. By the mid-1890s, mining had virtually ceased in the Cherry Creek area and the town had declined to a population of several hundred.

But it's hard to keep some mining towns down. In 1905, the district again revived. Ely's Nevada Northern Railway was extended through Cherry Creek in 1906, thereby linking the town with the outside world.

This revival lasted only about three years and by 1910, the town entered another decline. It perked up from 1933 to 1940, when the mines were once again reopened, but fell into another slump during and after the Second World War.

During the past decade, there has been small scale mining in the region, which has accounted for the town's continued existence.

A visit to Cherry Creek affords a good opportunity to see a relatively intact old and new Nevada mining camp. Newer homes, mostly plywood houses and mobile homes, are interspersed with the brick, stone, mud and wooden ruins of the older community.

In some cases, the newer construction has been added on to an original wooden cabin or house — creating a somewhat bizarre mixture of materials and design.

Wandering the dirt streets of Cherry Creek, you can find plenty of old remains of homes. For instance, the town contains one of the state's largest collections — I spotted at least a half-dozen — of unusual "sod homes" built by 19th century miners.

These houses were constructed partially into the ground or hillside and featured wooden beam roofs, over which sod or grass panels were placed. The result is a house that looks a little like a potato cellar, half-buried into the ground, with wooden doors and interior walls.

Other homes are tiny wooden shacks with corrugated metal roofs. In some cases, you can still see furnishings, including bed frames, mattresses, wooden tables and curtains, inside these build-ings.

These homes are also noteworthy because of the wonderful texture and appearance of their weathered, worn wooden walls. Behind nearly all of the two-dozen abandoned houses, you will also still find an outhouse, most in fairly good condition.

One of the most impressive of the ruins is a solid, red brick home, at the north end of the town, which, while in poor condi-tion, still has the remains of curtains fluttering through its broken windows. Inside, you can also see wallpaper on the walls and a few furnishings.

A handful of buildings scattered around the townsite indicate the influence of the railroad. These buildings, which include an old jail, are constructed of large, sturdy railroad ties.

In the center of the town, you can find the commercial district survivors, including a large red freight barn and the "Cherry Creek Barrel Saloon," an operating bar with considerable rustic charm, that even has a pay telephone.

Across the road from the red barn are the impressive remains of several stone buildings, again reminders of the rather substantial business district once located there. An historic marker adjacent to the ruins tells the Cherry Creek story.

On the westside of town, is the old Cherry Creek schoolhouse, still in good shape, which is now a local museum. Inside, you will find an assortment of antique bicycles, mining tools and furnish-ings collected from the area.

The museum is open from 10 a.m. to 5 p.m. on Saturdays and Sundays, from June to September.

On a hill south of the town, with a beautiful view of the sur-rounding Steptoe Valley, are at least three large cemeteries con-taining dozens of wooden and marble tombstones.

For more information, contact the Cherry Creek Museum, Star Route 1, Cherry Creek, NV, 89318, (702) 591-0411 or 591-9906. ❧

Angel Lake

Heavenly
Angel Lake

SOME OUT-OF-STATE PEOPLE assume that since Nevada is the driest state in the union, it must not have any lakes. Wrong.

In fact, Nevada has a number of lakes littered throughout its landscape that are quite beautiful. While most know of larger lakes, such as Tahoe, Pyramid and Mead, there are other, hidden lakes that offer scenery of equal beauty.

One of the best of these lesser-known "aqua gems" is Angel Lake, located in the East Humboldt Range near Wells. To reach Angel Lake, travel east on Interstate 80 to Wells, then follow the signs 12 miles to the lake via a good paved road.

Angel Lake must have received its name because it's so close to heaven — or maybe it just seems like it's that high in the mountains.

From Wells, the drive, while steep at times, is pleasant as you pass through rolling foothills of sagebrush and pinon pine. Climbing higher, the terrain changes. The pinion is replaced by mountain mahogany and, at about the 10 mile point, there is an impressive grove of zebra-stripped, quaking aspen that is intersected by the road.

Above and ahead is the crest of the East Humboldt Range. Like the nearby Ruby Mountains, which they resemble, the East Humboldts are among Nevada's most unique mountains. There is a timeless quality to these craggy ancient rocks; like the wizened face of a Basque bartender.

The mountains are fascinating. One minute the imposing

peaks seem like the jagged teeth of a giant bobcat and the next they are simply ragged stone upthrusts carved by time and the elements into uneven designs. Every time you look, they seem to be something different. Obvious yet still subtle.

If you look back toward Wells, you find a spectacular view of the surrounding rolling hills. A few miles before you reach Angel Lake, is the turn-off to Winchell Lake, a small reservoir perched on the side of the range. Signs also indicate a hiking trailhead.

The road finally begins to level as you get closer to Angel Lake. Adjacent to the lake is a small campground with a handful of sites and picnic tables.

The lake is not particularly large. Surrounded by rock walls on three sides (a manmade dam on the east side cups the water into a circular basin), Angel Lake resembles a glacial lake, which it was at one time.

The sheer walls appear to consist of a crumbly, cracked stone obviously shaped by the continual heating and cooling found at such high altitudes (the lake is at an elevation of 8,378 feet). Scarecrow limber pines hang on the mountain sides, barely surviving the harsh winters.

During a recent visit, the lake was being utilized by a couple of folks fishing as well as some well-equipped hikers who were embarking on the trails that lead across the Ruby Crest.

The trail runs south for miles along the west flank of the range. A sign indicates mileage to several points. It is 5 miles to Greys Lake, 11 miles to Ackler Creek, 18 miles to Boulder Lake and 25 to another trailhead at Pole Canyon.

An excellent source of information for hiking the East Humboldt and Ruby Mountains is "Hiking the Great Basin," By John Hart, published by Sierra Club Books. Additionally, the Wells Chamber of Commerce has produced a nice pamphlet.

For information, contact the Humboldt National Forest, (702) 752-3357. ❧

There's More
to Wendover Than
Salt and Sand

LOOKING ON MOST MAPS, it's easy to dismiss Wendover as simply the last place to play slot machines before hitting Utah The reality, however, is that there's much more to be found in this unique natural setting.

Located about a day's drive east of Reno via Interstate 80, Wendover, which is on the Nevada-Utah border, is perhaps best known for being the closest community to the famed Bonneville Salt Flats. These miles of flat, packed salt plains are the remains of ancient Bonneville Lake, a giant inland sea that once covered nearly all of Utah.

Decades ago, people discovered that the dry salt plains of Bonneville provided an incomparable surface for going fast. Over the years, a bushel of land speed records have been set on the Bonneville flats in just about anything that moves including rocket cars, motorcycles and bicycles.

The Bonneville Speed Museum in Wendover contains a nice

small collection of some of the vehicles, including several of the rocket-shaped jet cars that have, for at least a time, been the world's fastest thing on land. There is also an extensive collection of newspaper clippings and photographs detailing the many attempts to break the land speed records on the flats.

Additionally, the community of Wendover sponsors Speed Week each August, a celebration of acceleration. In recent years, several world records for smaller vehicles and bicycles have been set during Speed Week.

The unique topography of the Bonneville flats and surrounding area also provide another unusual opportunity. It is possible, after climbing the mountains to the west of Wendover, to actually see the curvature of the earth. The combination of flat ground stretching off for miles, clear air and lack of vegetation allows you to look out on the horizon and see the slight tilt of the earth.

The most accessible place to experience this phenomena is by driving west of Wendover for about three miles on the frontage road that parallels Interstate 80. There you will find a small mountain range which you can climb via several trails to a number of look-out points at the top.

The climb is also noteworthy because of the interesting shapes of the surrounding rocks, many of which look like broken stone bubbles — perhaps reflecting the fact the area was once under water.

Wendover is also notable because it was the location of a top secret airbase during the Second World War. It was at the Wendover base that the United States government stationed the 509th Composite Group that was responsible for flying the bombing missions over Japan that resulted in the dropping of the Atomic Bomb on Tokyo and Nagasaki.

An impressive stone and bronze monument has been erected adjacent to the Wendover Visitors Center, just off the interstate, to commemorate the men who worked on this project and as a monument to world peace.

Southeast of the main section of Wendover are the decaying remains of the Wendover airbase. Included are many of the old hangers that housed the airplanes of the 509th Composite Group during the war.

More recently, Wendover has experienced rapid growth as a tourism destination. With a half-dozen major casinos and highrise hotels, the town has become one of Nevada's more successful border boomtowns, attracting visitors from other states wishing to partake in Nevada-style fun.

Of special note, at the Stateline Hotel and Casino, is a small, but impressive slot machine collection, which includes more than a dozen ornate vintage one-armed bandits

For more information, contact Wendover USA, Box 2468, Wendover, NV 89883, (702) 664-3414. 🍃

Wendover

PART IV

The Great
Nevada
Southwest

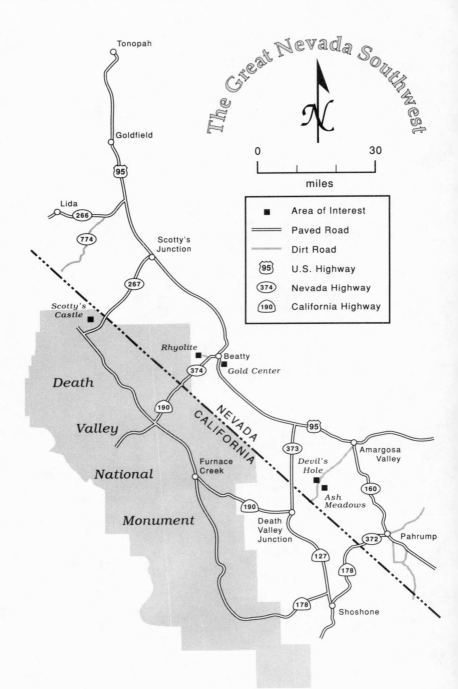

The Great
Nevada Southwest

YOU LOOK OUT ACROSS one of those big, dry valleys in southwestern Nevada and wonder how, in God's name, did those early pioneers survive in the days prior to air-conditioned automobiles? Directly west is the ominously-named Death Valley, while east is the restricted Nevada Testing Site — a place supposedly so remote and desolate that the federal government has determined it's only good for bombing.

Yet, despite what map-makers and our government have told us (and we know how trustworthy they can be), there is definitely something special about Nevada's southwestern corridor, a stretch that basically parallels modern Highway 95.

It remains a harsh land where you can stand on a hillside, looking down on the remains of some former mining camps such as Gold Center, Bullfrog or Rhyolite, and easily imagine one of those half-crazy desert rats — like Death Valley Scotty or Shorty Harris — trudging through the thick scrub, eyes scanning the remote landscape for the outcropping that just might produce the next Tonopah or Goldfield.

Mining was, and in some cases is, a big part of the story of this region. The highway roughly parallels the freight roads and railroad beds that once connected mining towns like Tonopah, Goldfield, Rhyolite and Carrera to railheads in places such as Las Vegas. While there are ghost towns found throughout the state (more on that in the next chapter), southwestern Nevada claims a disproportionate share of them.

Additionally, while most of it may look like miles of empty desert and dry mountains, the great Nevada southwest contains some of the most remarkable natural history sites in the western U.S. This is the home of Death Valley, a vast, natural petri dish of strange and unique biological, geological and environmental developments. Here you'll also find the rare, endangered pupfish, in places like Shoshone and Ash Meadows, as well as the more prolific wild burro, able to survive abandonment and the harsh elements.

The Nevada southwest is, without a doubt, the land of the unusual — where else can you find a castle in the desert, a river that flows underground and a fish so shy it can only spawn on a sunny ledge in a deep hole in the ground?

If you don't believe me, read on. . .

Grapevines and
Gourmet Dining
in Pahrump

THE IDEA OF A WINERY in Pahrump, Nevada seems about as likely as a dairy farm in downtown Las Vegas. But, it's there.

Bizarre as it sounds, in a field surrounded by miles of cheat grass and greasewood, stands a magnificent Spanish-style, white stucco winery — a kind of Chateau Sagebrush.

The Pahrump Valley Winery is the inspiration of Jack Sanders, a former Pahrump casino executive who believed the climate, soil and conditions in the Pahrump Valley were similar to the dry Temecula Valley grape-growing region near San Diego, California.

Sanders also discovered that a hundred years ago Nevada boasted a small grape-growing and wine-making region in the Pahrump.Valley. Historical records indicate those vines were eventually replaced with cotton and, more recently, with fields of alfalfa.

Sanders also found there had once been three bonded wineries in Nevada (his is number four). The identity of the first has been

135

lost, but the second was Chateau Buell in Pahrump, which produced a local wine of some repute. Its clients included the Furnace Creek Resort in Death Valley and the Los Angeles Athletic Club.

A third, called Bell Vista, apparently produced sacramental wines for Las Vegas churches from 1931-37.

With all that information in hand, Sanders decided the time was right for a Nevada winery. He broke ground on the $1.5 million winery in 1989 and, in July 1990, bottled his first wine. During the first year, he produced 26,000 bottles of wine.

During his first few years, Sanders says his wines will not be able to contain any juice from grapes grown in Pahrump.

"Grapes will grow here," he said. "But we're currently bringing grapes in from California."

His first batch of wine contained grapes from both the Monterey region (Grey Riesling) and Manteca area (French Columbard). He has planted some 10 acres of vines but it will take from three to four years before those grapes will be mature enough to be used for wine.

Ultimately, he plans to cultivate some 40 acres of grapes of several varieties, including "Symphony," a relatively new hybrid grape developed by the University of California at Davis that will thrive in drier climates.

To assist in producing the wines, Sanders sought a top name wine-maker and landed Demetri Tchelischeff, one of the country's best.

Under Tchelischeff's direction, the winery has released a number of wines, all with very distinctive, very-Nevada names. The sweetest is a wine called "Desert Rose," a fruity dinner wine with a touch of pink. Slightly drier is "Desert Blush," which Sanders calls a white zinfandel-type wine that is his best seller because of its "romantic name."

Slightly drier still is the Charleston Peak White, a tasty blend of Riesling and Columbard that Sanders describes as a pleasant everyday-type drinking wine.

In anticipation of producing his own "Symphony" wines, Sanders has also purchased California-grown "Symphony" grapes and produced a couple of wines, one slightly drier than the other, which have already won several awards. He is working on a Cabernet Sauvignon — one of his personal favorite wines — as well as other varietals.

Despite the newness of his winery, Sanders is already thinking of enlarging the facility because demand has outpaced capacity. At present, the winery can produce about 300,000 gallons of wine.

"We did not do this thing as a novelty — to have a winery in the desert," he said. "Remember wine was originally from the middle east and we plan to produce some terrific hot weather wines."

In addition to the winery, Sanders has also opened a first class gourmet restaurant in the building. With a limited seating capacity, the restaurant is doing a brisk business.

Sanders has also begun working on other expansion plans. He hopes to build a cheese factory adjacent to the winery and eventually there will be an outdoor amphitheater for concerts.

For more information, contact the Pahrump Valley Winery, 3810 Homestead Rd., Pahrump, NV 89041, (702) 727-6900. ❧

Pahrump Valley Winery

Ash Meadows

The Natural Wonders
of Ash Meadows

BIOLOGISTS AND BOTANISTS look at the broad expanses of
Nevada and, rather than see lots of empty spaces, recognize it is a
special environment teeming with unique fish, plant and animal
life.

One of the best of Nevada's "natural laboratories," filled with
hundreds of one-of-a-kind species of fish, plants and animals, is the
Ash Meadows Wildlife Refuge located in southwestern Nevada
about 25 miles south of Lathrop Wells, off Nevada State Route 373.

To reach Ash Meadows, head south on Highway 95 through
Tonopah. Lathrop Wells is located another two hours south of
Tonopah on 95.

Perhaps the first thing you notice about Ash Meadows is that
it looks like what most people think Nevada is; acres of sagebrush-
carpeted rolling hills occasionally populated by a stray juniper or
mesquite shrub. But, according to Larry Martin of the U.S. Fish
and Wildlife Service, there's much more to Ash Meadows.

"We have the greatest concentration of endemic species in the U.S.," Martin said. "Ash Meadows has 27 endemic species, including plants, fish and animal life that live only on the refuge and nowhere else."

Martin is one of a small staff of fish and wildlife employees responsible for the care and maintenance of Ash Meadows unique inhabitants.

He said the refuge, which encompasses about 24,000 acres, was originally part of a large Amargosa Valley alfalfa ranch, then later was used for cattle ranching.

In 1984, the Nature Conservancy purchased 12,000 acres for a refuge — largely to prevent further development. The land, and adjacent property, was acquired by the federal fish and wildlife department a few years later and staff was stationed on the refuge in 1987.

Martin said that Ash Meadows was acquired largely because of the presence of one rather special fish, the Devil's Hole Pupfish. This inch-long, almost transparent fish is only found in an ominously-named deep crevice in the ground, called Devil's Hole, which is located in the Ash Meadows area.

The Devil's Hole Pupfish also happens to be an endangered species. Martin said that the fish is only found in Devil's Hole and about 90 percent of the species lives within 20 feet of the water's surface, where they can spawn on a rock ledge and have access to sunlight.

As a result, water usage in the Amargosa Valley is carefully regulated to ensure that the water level in Devil's Hole doesn't drop. Martin said that scientists believe the springs in the Amargosa Valley — of which there are many — are fed by a common source and can be affected by changes in the area's water table.

Another unique aspect of Ash Meadows is that it includes a half-dozen or so geothermal spring-fed pools and each boasts its own species of pupfish. For example, the Ash Meadows Amargosa Pupfish thrives in Crystal Springs and the Warm Springs Pupfish can be found at the aptly-named Warm Springs.

Martin said that each pool was probably once part of a larger body of water but eventually receded into smaller, separate ponds in which each group of pupfish evolved differently.

"Most of the species out here are endangered or threatened," Martin noted. "In addition to the pupfish, we've identified seven unique species of plants, 10 species of snail and two species of insects."

Walking through the refuge is a wonderfully peaceful experience. A few hundred yards from the road it's not uncommon to spot wild horses and burros slowly foraging through the area — all remarkably unafraid.

Crystal Springs is perfectly named with its sparkling, inviting clear waters. Standing on the grassy edge of the warm spring-fed pond (temperatures run about 85 degrees), which is about the size of a small swimming pool, you can see small bubbles rising from somewhere below, then gurgle to the surface.

Peering into the water you can see the tiny pupfish swimming around a rock ledge, looking like miniature transparent sardines.

Among the remnants of the old cattle ranch are two larger manmade lakes, fed by overflow from the springs. On one, Crystal Lake, swimming and boating are allowed.

Martin points out, however, that the lakes are an exception to the general rule that the refuge should be as close to its original state as possible. With that in mind, the federal agency is trying to reestablish marshes and put the springs back in their original channels.

For more information, contact the U.S. Department of Fish and Wildlife at (702) 372-5435. ❧

Shoshone

Shoshone
Stone Condos

THE TINY TOWN OF SHOSHONE, located on the California-Nevada border, is generally known for one thing — it's the closest place to Las Vegas to buy California lottery tickets.

But there are a couple of other interesting things about Shoshone that make it worthy of a visit. For one, the entire town is owned by Susan Sorrells, a descendent of one of the tiny hamlet's founders, who has helped it avoid the oblivion of most old mining camps.

Additionally, the community boasts a row of miners' homes carved into nearby rock cliffs nearly a century ago. The small stone cubicles — which resemble latter-day pueblo dwellings — frequently included square-cut window holes and even shelves carved in the walls.

Shoshone is located about 33 miles west of Pahrump in the southern part of the state via Nevada State Route 372 and California State Route 178.

The miners' stone homes sit west of the main part of Shoshone in a small canyon lined by sandstone cliffs, in which the structures were cut.

The homes are another example of the unusual building materials used to construct housing in early 20th century mining camps. Because of the scarcity of brick and wood, miners frequently turned to more inventive materials, including bottles, cardboard, canvas, sod and, in the case of Shoshone, sandstone.

Wandering through Shoshone's rock condos is interesting. Inside, the homes are surprisingly roomy and cool. Most have stovepipe holes cut into the ceilings, showing that stoves were common. A few even have the rusted remains of bedframes (as well as plenty of other garbage, indicating the all-too-common effects of neglect and vandalism).

One of the apartments was built on two levels, kind of a two-story stone townhouse. Cut steps lead from the lower level to the upper floor.

Additionally, the miners weren't much for cleanliness. The center of the valley area is littered with the rusted remains of cans and other assorted garbage.

Rather than develop a garbage area away from their homes, the miners used to toss their trash out the front door into the sagebrush and locals have kept the site in its original condition. A quarter mile from the miner's housing development is a frontier cemetery.

The rest of Shoshone consists of some half-dozen buildings, including a motel, convenience store, restaurant, real estate office and local museum.

The latter offers a glimpse into the community's past. Originally built in 1906 in another mining town called Greenwater, the building was moved in 1922 to Shoshone by Susan Sorrells' great grandfather.

Over the years the white-washed wooden building served as a

garage, gas station and general store before being converted into a museum. Adjacent to the museum is an adobe building that was once a boarding house for the old Tonopah and Tidewater Railroad.

Sorrells, who has been featured in several national magazines, inherited the 1,000-acres that make up Shoshone about a decade ago when her mother died. After growing up in the area, she had attended schools in the east and was living in Europe when she was called home.

A trim, elegant woman in her 40s, Sorrells recalled that the town quickly grew on her and she decided to stay. Over the years, she has fought attempts to radically change her town, including several lucrative offers to convert it into a mini-Furnace Creek type resort on the edge of Death Valley.

Instead, she has attempted to retain the town's sleepy quality while also developing appropriate new industries, including commercial catfish ponds that utilize the natural hot springs in the area.

Sorrells is most proud of the fact that these ponds are also the home of the Shoshone pupfish, a species once thought extinct until she began cleaning the ponds.

For more information about Shoshone, contact the Shoshone Development Company, (619) 852-4302. ❧

Furnace Creek Ranch

Winter is
Death Valley Time

PART ONE

DEATH VALLEY MAY BE ONE OF THE DRIEST, hottest, most desolate pieces of real estate in the world, but when frost appears on your windshield, snow dusts the mountains and you can see your breath outside, it starts to look pretty inviting.

Winter is Death Valley time. While home may be below the freezing point, average Death Valley temperatures in the winter months "dip" from the 50s and 60s in December to the 70s in April — and frequently are higher. In the summer, however, temperatures can rise into the 130s, so beware.

The Death Valley National Monument is located along Nevada's western border.

Of course, escaping cold weather isn't the only reason to visit Death Valley. Despite its arid, barren appearance, Death Valley is actually a fascinating and beautiful place to visit, filled with historic sites, unique natural areas and a remarkable array of recreational opportunities.

147

Death Valley gets a bad rap because of its unpleasant name and the horrible-sounding names of many of the landmarks found there. For instance, the mountains bordering Nevada are called the Funeral Mountains, the lowest point is called Badwater and the best place to stay is called Furnace Creek. All sound pretty appealing, don't they?

Historians tell us that Death Valley was first settled by roaming tribes of native Americans, including the Shoshone. In 1849, a group of white settlers entered the valley, thinking it was a shortcut to California.

After barely surviving the trek across the area, these hardy pioneers coined the name, Death Valley.

Today, travelers in air-conditioned automobiles can have a much more pleasant experience. A modern visitors center operated by the National Park Service at Furnace Creek is probably the best place to start any tour of the area.

Located in the center of Death Valley, the visitors center offers an informative 18-minute video presentation and displays describing the history of the area. The center is also well stocked with books, tapes, pamphlets and videos about the region which can be purchased.

The Furnace Creek Ranch Resort, adjacent to the visitors center, is, along with Furnace Creek Inn, the only privately-owned land in the national monument and is a true oasis in the desert. Visitors will find restaurants, a gas station, a general store, horseback riding, a golf course and rustic cabins.

The Borax Museum on the ranch describes this colorful part of the area's history. Borax is part of a family of chemical compounds used in the production of glass, porcelain enamel, soap, ceramics and fertilizers.

In the 1870s, prospectors discovered large deposits of Borates in the salt flats of Death Valley. In the 1880s, large scale mining operations developed in the valley. To haul the ore to nearby refineries, the mines began using 20-mule teams, which were the only animals hardy enough to survive in the desert. These mule trains were later made famous in Borax advertisements.

While there are still borate reserves in Death Valley, nearly all mining has ceased in the region because it is no longer cost effective.

The Borax Museum highlights the unique minerals and mining equipment from that era. Just north of Furnace Creek Ranch are the remains of the historic Eagle and Harmony Borax Works, which visitors are free to explore.

While Furnace Creek Ranch is like an elaborate dude ranch, visitors seeking something a bit more civilized can stay at Furnace Creek Inn, a magnificent 1930s resort located a few miles southeast of the ranch, overlooking Death Valley.

Guests here find an intriguing elegance — jackets are required at dinner — reminiscent of the era of the Great Gatsby. The four-star inn resembles a stone and stucco Spanish-style castle on the hill, surrounded by lush landscaping.

The ranch and inn also offer 110 shaded RV spaces with services, and another 1,000 undeveloped spaces offered by the National Park Service.

Room rates at both the ranch and inn vary depending on time of year and day of the week. For more information, contact Furnace Creek Inn and Ranch reservations, (800) 528-6367 (good throughout the U.S.). ❧

Zabriskie Point

Death Valley's Scenic Wonders

PART TWO

WHILE PLACES LIKE FURNACE CREEK make a stay in Death Valley more pleasurable, the real show is found at the great number of incomparable natural scenic areas located there.

Many of the Death Valley National Monument's scenic wonders are accessible by car, but there are also some incredible natural sights found on hiking trails that criss-cross the 3,000 square miles within the monument boundaries

Starting at the north end of Death Valley (driving in via Nevada State Route 267) you pass Scotty's Castle, an impressive Spanish-style mansion built between 1922 and 1933 by a Chicago millionaire. Tours of the castle are offered daily.

From the castle, the road continues southwest into Death Valley through the scenic Grapevine Canyon. About eight miles from Scotty's is Ubehebe Crater, a unique geological formation created more than 1,000 years ago when a volcano erupted.

The road to the crater takes you right to the rim. From here you can see a huge divet in the ground — as if God missed that first swing with the celestial 9-iron — that measures about a half-mile wide and 750-feet deep.

Returning to the main road (now California State Route 190), there is a drive of 52 miles to the Stovepipe Wells historic site and adjacent sand dunes. Here you will find some beautiful sand mounds created over centuries out of rock particles blown into this valley from the Cottonwood Mountains to the west and northwest.

The dunes take on a variety of shapes, influenced by the strong winds that whip across the valley. As with the sand dunes found in Nevada, the area was once part of a giant lake. The sand sits atop an old clay playa; the mounds interrupted in places by white salt deposits.

Southwest of the dunes is Stovepipe Wells Village, the only commercially developed area, besides Furnace Creek, in the monument. Visitors will find accommodations, camping, recreational vehicle parking, restaurants, a gas station and a general store.

Heading west of Stovepipe Wells takes you to the Emigrant Ranger Station and the Emigrant Canyon drive. This scenic drive takes you to Aguereberry Point, which offers a splendid view of Death Valley from about 6,400-feet.

If you continue south through Emigrant Canyon, you can also reach the historic Wildrose Charcoal Kilns.

If you continue directly south of the dunes on Highway 190, you pass through Furnace Creek and can either veer east back toward Nevada via Death Valley Junction (north to Lathrop Wells or south to Pahrump) or head to the southern portion of Death Valley.

The former trip takes you to famous Zabriskie Point, one of the many geological marvels of Death Valley. At the point, the scenery, while familiar and sometimes crowded, remains impressive. From here, you can look west into the Death Valley flats and admire the surrounding photogenic clay canyons delicately carved by nature's tools.

A few miles east of Zabriskie Point is an interesting side road called "Twenty Mule Team Canyon." This one-way, one-lane trail takes you through the heart of Borax country.

The tan-colored terrain appears to have the consistency of dried mud and looks like mounds of collapsed adobe. Throughout the canyon, you can still see dark entrances to the many Borax mines that once operated here.

About 25 miles from the Twenty Mule Team Canyon is Dante's View, a spot about 5,500-feet above Death Valley that offers perhaps the best view of the region.

If you head to the southern portion of the monument, south of Furnace Creek on Highway 178, you can travel to a number of other fascinating places, including Gold Canyon, Artists Palette, Devil's Golf Course and Badwater.

Gold Canyon is an interpretive road that takes you to the Red Cathedral, an unusual red-colored stone formation. Artists Palette is a one-way loop road through an old lake bed that offers an opportunity to view marvelous brightly-colored red, brown, green and yellow cliffs and hills. The vivid shades are the result of oxidation of minerals in the sediments.

Devil's Golf Course, about six miles south of Artists Palette, is another highlight of the monument. The salt crystals that cover the ground are almost pure table salt (remains of the ancient lake that once covered the area) and the surrounding pinnacles have been shaped into interesting designs.

Badwater, a few miles farther south, is the lowest elevation you can drive to in the western hemisphere (nearly 280-feet below sea level).

From here, if you continue south, then east, it is about 150 miles to Las Vegas via Pahrump.

The Death Vally Visitor Center at Furnace Creek has a number of useful guidebooks and maps, including suggested day and half-day trips. For more information about the Death Valley National Monument, call (619) 786-2331. ✌

Scotty's Castle

Death Valley Scotty's Private Castle

W HEN YOU FIRST SEE SCOTTY'S CASTLE, you almost have to rub your eyes to make sure you're not looking at a mirage.

Perched on the northeastern edge of desolate Death Valley, Scotty's Castle is a fabulous testimonial to the fact that you can build anything — including a veritable castle in the desert — if you've got the desire and money.

Built in the early 1920s as a vacation getaway by a wealthy insurance magnate named Albert M. Johnson, the castle is a kind of mini-San Simeon filled with antiques, history and unusual, ahead-of-their-time architectural designs.

The story behind the castle is intriguing. Just after the turn of the century, a colorful miner named Walter E. Scott — or "Death Valley Scotty" — who had spent many years prospecting in the Rhyolite-Death Valley area, befriended Albert Johnson.

Stories indicate that Scotty suggested Grapevine Canyon as the site for Johnson's vacation castle. The location had water and a commanding view of Death Valley. Soon, a massive Spanish-style stucco and tile mansion was built on the desert's edge.

Albert Johnson spared no expense in creating his castle. Elaborate turrets rise above the dozens of rooms in the compound. Inside, he filled the place with rustic southwestern furniture, wall hangings and decor.

During nine years of construction — the castle eventually cost between $1.5 and $2 million in 1920s dollars — Johnson also incorporated a few unique design features. For instance, there is a ceiling to floor waterfall in the front room. In addition to its aesthetic qualities, the purpose of the waterfall is to help cool the room — remember this home was built before air-conditioning.

Additionally, Albert Johnson experimented with a series of fans blowing air across large ice blocks into an underground vent system — another attempt at air-conditioning — as well as with an early version of a solar heating system.

When the complex was completed, the Johnsons named it the Death Valley Ranch. However, Albert Johnson also had a good sense of humor. As Scotty was a frequent guest, the two would often tell people that Scotty was the proprietor and Johnson was simply a visitor. Within a short time, most people referred to the facility as "Scotty's Castle" rather than its real name (park ranger guides note that for years many believed that Scotty was the owner and built it from his mining earnings).

By the late 1920s, the castle had become a haven for America's celebrities, with the Johnsons and their official "host," Scotty, entertaining dozens of the original rich and famous.

An informative tour takes you through the exotic front room (with waterfall) and the enormous dining room and kitchen, then through the guest rooms, including Scotty's personal chambers (highlight of this room is a rather special hole in the wall — don't forget to ask for the story behind the hole).

You will also see the large garage (complete with a vintage

1920s car), which once housed the shiny big vehicles of the stars who were frequent guests, including Will Rogers and Cecil B. DeMille.

The castle complex was never completed because Albert Johnson's fortune was diminished during the Great Depression in the 1930s. Visitors will see the partially built swimming pool adjacent to the house as well as an interesting tower, also not quite finished, which was to house a power plant.

After Johnson's death in 1948, Scotty was allowed to live at the ranch for the remainder of his life. He died in 1954.

The home, which was given in Mrs. Johnson's will to a religious group, remained open for tours during the 1950s and 60s. In 1970, the U.S. Government acquired the castle and incorporated it into the Death Valley National Monument.

Scotty's Castle is located about an hour northwest of Beatty via U.S. Highway 95 and State Route 267. The castle is operated by the National Park Service, which offers daily regular tours and publishes an excellent map brochure about Death Valley and Scotty's Castle.

For information, contact the Superintendent, Death Valley National Monument, Death Valley, CA 92328, (619) 786-2331. ❧

Beatty Stone Cutters

Hard Rock
Beatty

MANY PEOPLE DRIVING on U.S. Highway 95 from Reno to Las Vegas know the town of Beatty as simply the place where you get gas and maybe grab a sandwich before tackling the last two hours of the trip.

But for those who take the time to stop and smell the sagebrush, Beatty actually has a bit of history to it and is home of one of Nevada's most unique businesses, the Nevada Neanderthal Stone Company.

Contrary to appearances, Beatty did not spring to life as an RV park. While the history books are a little sketchy, the area is believed to have been originally settled in 1870 by a man named Landers. All that seems to be known about Mr. Landers is that he built a small stone cabin adjacent to a bubbling spring.

In 1896, Montillus Murray Beatty acquired the Landers ranch and moved into the stone cabin. He planted trees around the structure and cultivated a variety of crops.

When gold was discovered over the hill in the Bullfrog mining district (so named because of the unusual green color of the ore), Beatty's ranch was ideally located and, more importantly, had plenty of water from the Amargosa River, which runs underground through the area. Indeed, the area around the ranch was named Oasis Valley.

The town of Beatty was established in 1904, south of the ranch. It quickly became an important supply point for surrounding mining towns like Bullfrog and Rhyolite, and survived because it was located on the shortest route between the booming mining town of Goldfield and the railroad yards of Las Vegas.

Beatty sold his ranch and springs in 1906 and moved into the growing town of Beatty, which, by that time, boasted 1,000 residents and a major hotel, the 23-room Montgomery Hotel. He died two years later at the age of 73, after suffering an injury while hauling wood.

In 1906, a rail line was completed that linked Beatty to Las Vegas, and the following year a line was built connecting the town to Goldfield.

The Bullfrog mining boom ended as quickly as it began, with most mines shutting down by 1909. Beatty, while experiencing a substantial drop in population, was able to survive because of the same things that first attracted people there; availability of water and location on a major highway.

Today, visitors find a pleasant small community with three fairly large casinos (the Exchange Club, the Burro Inn and the Stagecoach), several RV parks, a developed hot springs (Bailey's, located six miles north of town) and about a half-dozen gas stations.

In recent years, Beatty has become popular with the RV crowd, attracted by the comfortably warm, winter weather and proximity to Death Valley.

Additionally, Beatty is gaining some measure of notoriety

because of the work of Dave Spicer and his team of stone-cutters at Nevada Neanderthal Stone Company, located just outside of town.

Tall, trim, clean-cut and bespectacled, with a can of chewing tobacco tucked in this blue-jeans, the youthful Spicer looks more like a mining geologist than a budding entrepreneur. But after only a few years in business, he has been able to rack up impressive annual sales selling custom-cut stone.

He has already collared some pretty impressive clients, including Steve Wynn, owner of the new Mirage Hotel in Las Vegas, who commissioned two white stone elephants for his resort (they're located in the white tiger display).

Spicer's operation is all home-grown, including the stone. He cuts it at a quarry located about five miles from his shop, and describes it as an igneous white pumice rock known as Rhyolite Tuft.

"It was just a wild-assed idea and we've learned alot since we started," Spicer said modestly.

While most of the crew, including Spicer, is self-taught (only the master stone-cutter, George Taylor, had any previous experience), their work is impressive. Visitors can tour the plant or wander through an interesting stone garden showing how the stone can be cut and used.

For more information, contact the Beatty Chamber of Commerce, P.O. Box 946, Beatty, NV 89003, (702) 553-2424. ✒

Gold Center

All That Glitters
is Not Gold

IT'S AMAZING THE NUMBER of Nevada mining towns that popped up almost overnight, then disappeared even faster.

Most of these "now-you-see-them-now-you-don't" towns were frequently little more than tent cities, but a few, such as Gold Center, were able to claim at least a few brick and stone buildings before vanishing.

The remains of Gold Center are located three miles south of Beatty, on a hillside directly west of U.S. Highway 95.

Despite its name, Gold Center wasn't the location of any successful mining and never produced any gold. Indeed, its sole reason for being was the Amargosa River, which runs adjacent to the former site. The town supplied water to the surrounding mines and mining communities.

In 1904, a townsite was laid out and named Gold Center. The town's optimistic developers hoped that Gold Center would surpass nearby Bullfrog and other mining camps as a kind of mining camp suburb (you know the sales pitch — "live in Gold Center so you don't have to live where you work").

When the Las Vegas & Tonopah Railroad was constructed through the area in 1906, Gold Center was selected as its connection with the nearby mines. Unfortunately, that was just about the high point in Gold Center's existence.

Less than a year later, rail facilities were completed to Rhyolite, which had grown much larger, and Gold Center began to lose its importance.

The end, however, wasn't immediate. A large brewery and ice plant was constructed in Gold Center in 1907, as were several dozen wooden homes and a number of businesses, such as a post office, bank, hotel, stores, saloons and newspaper office.

Additionally, a large mining mill was erected on the hillside above the town to process ore from the district. A mining company even sank several shafts in adjacent hills to test the area for mineral potential, but found nothing noteworthy.

All proved to be bad investments. By the time the Bullfrog mines went bust and Rhyolite began to fail, about 1910, Gold Center was already declining and quickly evaporated into the warm desert air.

A visitor today will find only a few reminders of Gold Center. Much of the former site has been destroyed by dredge mining operations during the past few decades.

The best remains are found on the hillside overlooking a large pond of water diverted from the Amargosa. This scene is somewhat interesting because the pond still has a large, rusting yellow dredging machine at its south end.

Wandering through the stone and brick ruins on the hillside, you can find the large, rusted, round bottoms of a couple of metal tanks once part of the mill. In addition, you can find stone foundations, cracked concrete floors and the intriguing remnants of some kind of brick and iron oven.

About six miles farther south, to the east of Highway 95, are the remains of Carrera, another early 20th century mining town. Unlike most of the state's mining camps, Carrera didn't develop because of gold or silver, but due to the presence of marble.

Carrera, which was named for the famed Italian marble district, was founded in about 1911, after significant marble deposits were discovered in a canyon directly east of the townsite.

A small town developed in 1913, which eventually included a post office, stores, hotel and a community swimming pool (water was piped from Gold Center). A small railroad spur line was built linking a railroad station in the town to the canyon quarries, about four miles into the mountains.

But marble mining eventually proved to be unprofitable and operations were shut down in the early 1920s. The town began a rapid decline and has essentially disappeared.

Today, visitors will find a few concrete foundations adjacent to the highway. About a mile east of the highway, a few hundred yards from the dirt road leading to the former quarry, you can also find a partial chimney and other remains of another building, perhaps a house or part of the hotel.

Another interesting historic footnote is that, about a mile-and-a-half north of Carrera, you will see three or four concrete structures standing in the desert. These buildings, which are not part of Carrera, are the remnants of a concrete plant built in the mid-1930s.

For more information, contact the Beatty Chamber of Commerce, Box 940, Beatty, NV 89003, (702) 553-2424. ❧

Amargosa Opera House

Marta Becket's Dream

"I do not plan for the years ahead. I don't try to attempt to guess what I will be able to do ten years from now. At present, I dance . . ."

— Marta Becket

MARTA BECKET LIVES FOR DANCING. Indeed, since February 10, 1968, she has chosen to do her unique brand of classical ballet and other dance in a former mining town community hall, built in 1924, located virtually in the middle of nowhere. And she wouldn't have it any other way.

The story of Marta Becket and her Amargosa Opera House is a fascinating profile of someone who found the freedom to pursue her dream in the most unlikely of places — the Nevada-Eastern California Mohave Desert.

Still trim and athletic at age 68, the attractive, dark-haired

Becket recalls discovering her future opera house, located at Death Valley Junction, quite by accident.

"In 1967, we were vacationing in Death Valley," she said. "One morning we woke up to find we had a flat tire on our trailer. From one of the park rangers there we learned the best place to have it repaired was Death Valley Junction."

Upon arriving in the hamlet, which consisted of little more than a gas station and a strange U-shaped complex of Mexican Colonial-style buildings, her then-husband, Tom Williams, began fixing the tire, while she decided to explore the town.

The town had been founded in 1907 by the Pacific Coast Borax Company. Most of the buildings had been built from 1923-24 as part of a company town that included company offices, a general store, dormitory, hotel and recreation hall.

She came to the small, crumbling former recreation hall, on the northeast end of the complex ,and walked around back. Through a small hole in a door, she peered inside to see a small stage draped with a worn curtain, rows of wooden benches and plenty of debris.

She thought it was the most beautiful thing she'd ever seen.

Becket had spent more than 20 years dancing in New York, including with the corps de ballet at Radio City Music Hall and in a number of Broadway productions, including, "Showboat," "A Tree Grows in Brooklyn," "Wonderful Town" and her own concert tours.

By 1967, however, musical tastes had changed and Becket says she was finding it harder to survive as a solo performer on tour. She remembers being discouraged, tired and filled with uncertainty about the future — and sorely in need of a break — when her husband had suggested a desert vacation.

She showed him the decrepit town hall building and her ideas began to spill out. She envisioned an opera house, where she could continue to perform, continue to dance.

Twenty years before Kevin Costner ever discovered his "Field of Dreams," she'd heard her own voice tell her, "If you build it they will come."

No fan of life in New York, Tom Williams also saw the possibilities and the two set out to make this shaky proposition a reality. They rented the theater, repaired the leaky roof, painted the walls, sewed a curtain and costumes and opened for business.

"On opening night, we had 12 people," she said. "But the audiences started to grow and the publicity reached a point where you now need reservations during the season.

"I had no idea this would happen. I just wanted to extend myself."

She recalls that her New York friends thought she was crazy to forego life in the Big Apple for subsistence in the big sandpile — but she persevered and, ultimately, thrived.

Becket estimates she performs before some 12,000 people each year, during a season that runs from October to May. Among those who have attended her one-woman performances over the past 24 seasons have been actors Marlon Brando and Lew Ayres as well as writer Ray Bradbury.

Performances include three programs of original ballet-mimes, during which Becket will assume several dozen roles. Last year's season featured, "A Viennese Valentine" or "Cupid's Mistake," "Curtain Raiser" and "The Second Mortgage."

In addition to performing, Becket is an accomplished painter, who has illustrated several books as well as painted the backdrops for her programs. While her works have been exhibited in galleries in New York, perhaps her most ambitious project was the interior of the Opera House, which sports a massive wall and ceiling mural.

The impressive, Renaissance-influenced painting, which she worked on from 1968 to 1974, depicts a 16th century opera audience, including a king and queen, as well as entertainers ranging from Native Americans to characters from her favorite operas.

Along the way, with the help of supporters, Becket's Amargosa Opera House, Inc., a non-profit association, has also been able to purchase the Opera House and much of the town of Death Valley Junction, to ensure its survival. In 1981, it was listed in the National Register of Historic Places.

While she won't predict how much longer she will be able to continue following her muse, fortunately for us, Becket plans at least a few more seasons.

The Amargosa Opera House is located about 50 miles south-west of Beatty, Nevada, via U.S. Highway 95 and State Route 373. It sits in the tiny enclave of Death Valley Junction, on the edge of the Death Valley National Monument, about eight miles from the Nevada-California border on California State Route 127 (which connects to Route 373).

Performances are scheduled on Saturday evenings at 8:15 p.m. during October, December and mid-May; and Friday, Saturday and Monday evenings at 8:15 p.m. during November, January, February, March and April. Cost is $8 for adults and $5 for children under 12.

For more information, contact the Amargosa Opera House, Death Valley Junction, CA 92328, (619) 852-4316. ❧

PART V

A Fading Heritage:

Nevada's Ghost Towns

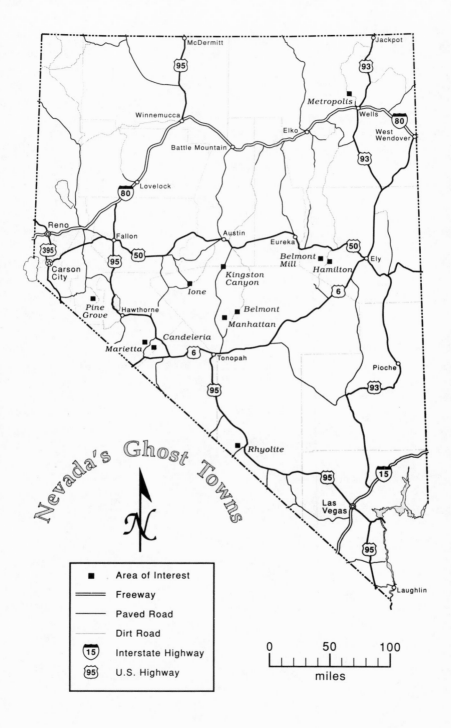

Nevada's Ghost Towns

| McDermitt | Jackpot |
| Winnemucca | Metropolis |
| Wells |
| Elko | West Wendover |
| Battle Mountain |
| Lovelock |
Reno	Austin	Eureka
Fallon	Belmont Mill
Carson City	Hamilton	Ely
Kingston Canyon
Pine Grove	Ione
Hawthorne	Belmont
Candeleria	Manhattan
Marietta	Tonopah	Pioche
Rhyolite
Las Vegas
Laughlin

Legend:
- ■ Area of Interest
- Freeway
- Paved Road
- Dirt Road
- (15) Interstate Highway
- (95) U.S. Highway

0   50   100
miles

A Fading Heritage: Nevada's Ghost Towns

I LOVE EXPLORING GHOST TOWNS and hate what has happened to many of them. If circumstances don't dramatically change in the next few years, I don't expect that there will be too much left to see at most of Nevada's ghost towns by the early part of the next century.

Much of the decay and degradation of these historic sites is natural; the result of neglect and the often harsh Nevada environment. Others, however, have been vandalized, damaged, ripped off for souvenirs or destroyed purposely in the name of progress.

A sad reality is that it's tough to round up the resources for historic sites, particularly when they are located in places where no one lives. The "Catch 22" of the situation is, of course, that the paucity of people is what makes it unique and worth preserving, yet the lack of people means there's no political constituency to pursue the necessary preservation.

Additionally, the same reasons that originally attracted people to many of these areas — namely the presence of some kind of minerals — are now threatening a few of these towns. Over the past few years, newer mining efforts, which are usually large open pit operations, have obliterated some ghost town sites. In other cases, most notably the town of Tuscarora, local residents have had some measure of success in preserving an historic community.

If there's any message I would like to pass on regarding Nevada's ghost towns and historic sites, it's that everyone should respect these fragile, irreplaceable treasures. Feel free to take photos and admire the ruins but please don't use metal detectors to dig up the sites or remove anything, no matter how insignificant it might seem.

Nevada's ghost towns are part of what defines the state. In most cases, these towns owe their brief existences to mining, which was a major impetus for the state's earliest settlement, as well as one of the reasons it was accepted into the union of United States in 1864.

These historic, once-flourishing mining camps — there are hundreds of them — can be found almost everywhere in the state. Some never grew to more than tent cities, with a few hundred people, while others exploded into major communities with thousands of residents, before fading and, in some cases, disappearing.

The following stories highlight about a dozen ghost towns I've been privileged to visit and explore. Obviously, there are many more — this is not intended to be an all-inclusive listing. Additionally, readers of the first "Backyard Traveler" book recall that it featured a few of the more well-known ghost towns, including Goldfield, Gold Point, Berlin, Sutro, Como and Unionville.

The ghost towns that follow range from towns that were truly no more than historical footnotes, such as Pine Grove, Belmont Mill, Marietta, Kingston and Ione, to more significant and substantial communities, like Rhyolite, Hamilton, Manhattan, Candelaria and Belmont.

Also included is a brief look at the optimistically-named Metropolis, an early 20th century agricultural community that never realized its potential.

And lest anyone might think nothing is being done to preserve historic sites in the state, it should be noted that the Nevada Office of Historic Preservation and the Nevada Cultural Affairs Commission as well as a handful of private preservation groups (Preservation Association of Clark County, Comstock Historic District Commission, Friends of Rhyolite and others) are doing what they can to at least ensure some piece of Nevada's history will survive for the next generation.

Belmont Survives

THE SMELL OF SAGEBRUSH IS STRONG while the sun, in the home stretch, casts long shadows on the brick and stone remains of Belmont, the ghost town that refuses to disappear.

Founded in 1865, Belmont is one of Nevada's oldest and most historic communities. Despite its abandonment nearly a century ago, Belmont has somehow defied the odds — yielding to many of the ravages of time and careless destruction, but hanging on to its existence while other, younger towns have become little more than memories.

Belmont is located 43 miles northeast of Tonopah via U.S. Highway 6 and State Route 376.

A visit to Belmont is a chance to view one of the most intact ghost towns in the state. With more than a dozen buildings sprouting out of the sagebrush, including a partially restored red brick courthouse, and a number of substantial ruins, Belmont looks and feels like a ghost town.

At the western boundary of the town, you reach the first two historic sites. To the south is the shaded town cemetery, which contains a handful of hand-carved wooden markers.

North of the cemetery are the remains of the Belmont-Monitor Mill, one of several mills erected in the area in the 1870s. At the mill site, you can wander through extensive brick ruins, highlighted by a 15-foot brick smokestack.

East of the Belmont-Monitor Mill site is the main part of the town. Newer homes have been built around the ruins during the

175

past couple of years, indicating that Belmont is a "living" ghost town.

The Belmont Saloon, open during the summer months, is Belmont's only active business. Inside, visitors will find an historic backbar — originally in Belmont's Cosmopolitan Saloon — and other artifacts from the town's past (also a great antique player piano).

Adjacent to the saloon, you will find a picturesque row of dilipidated brick and wooden storefronts. This classic ghost town scene is one of the most photographed in the state.

Sadly, a few years ago, vandals knocked down the historic Cosmopolitan Saloon, which used to stand on the main street. You can still find the flattened remnants of the two-story, wooden building.

Just beyond the main section on a knoll overlooking the town is the Belmont Courthouse. This impressive two-story building was constructed in 1876 from brick manufactured in Belmont's own kilns as a cost of $25,000.

The courthouse was Nye County's original county building and was used until 1905 when Belmont lost the county seat to Tonopah. It eventually fell into disrepair, but was acquired by the Nevada Division of State Parks in the 1970s and partially restored.

At the east end of the old mining camp, one of the town's original stone houses has been rebuilt into a beautiful residence.

If you head south of the main section, following the road just over a hill, you will find other important ruins, including the remains of one of the original brick kilns (including an impressive 20-foot red smokestack rising from a former brick oven).

About a quarter mile west of the brick oven, is the Highbridge Mill site. The two-story building retains its large, nine-window brick facade, as well as the massive sidewalls.

History books record that high grade silver ore was discovered in the Belmont area in 1865. The district originally was called Silver Bend, then Philadelphia, before taking the name Belmont.

The presence of large trees in the surrounding Monitor Range, as well as clay and water, allowed residents to construct more permanent structures than most mining camps.

In 1867, Belmont was named the Nye County seat and had become a regional center for trading, milling and mining. In addition to commercial businesses, a school, bank and post office were established and the town claimed two newspapers.

By 1868, the population of Belmont had risen to 2,000, but the next year decline began as other mining areas proved more profitable. A second strike in 1873, revitalized the town and again boosted the population.

By 1887, however, the mines began to decline and by the turn of the century, Belmont could support only a handful of businesses. The mills finally ground to a halt during World War I and Belmont began its slumber.

For more information, contact the Nevada Division of State Parks, (702) 687-4384. 🙣

Belmont

Belmont Mill

Overlooked Belmont Mill

THE WIND WHISTLES LOUDLY through loose-fitting tin-sheeted walls and a bird shrieks irritably at an intruder. It's obvious that it has been a long time since anyone has visited the remains of Belmont Mill, one of the best preserved of Nevada's early 20th century mining camps.

Few Nevada mining history books even mention Belmont Mill, which is not to be confused with the famous mining town of Belmont, located north of Tonopah. Belmont Mill was developed during a mining boom in White Pine County in 1915.

Belmont Mill is located about seven miles southwest of the ghost town of Hamilton. To reach it, head 37 miles west of Ely on Highway 50, then turn south on the marked road to Hamilton. Drive 10 miles on a maintained dirt road, then follow the signs (adjacent to the Hamilton Cemetery) to Belmont Mill. There will be a fork in the road about two miles from Hamilton, turn left to reach the site.

The main mining mill building is quite impressive, sitting on a hillside overlooking a narrow canyon. The structure is largely intact, perhaps because it was constructed of thick metal sheets attached to a sturdy wooden frame. It is obvious that the builders intended for this structure to last.

Peeking inside the main building — and be careful not to touch anything or go inside because the wooden floors don't appear too safe — you can still see the milling equipment and a variety of other mining paraphernalia.

You can also still find large elevated wooden bins filled with rocks on the south side of the mill. Apparently, these carts served as counter-weights to lift the ore containers to the top of the mill, where the precious dirt and rocks were dumped into the mill for processing.

Also intact is an aerial tramway (which resembles the kind of aerial lift you find today at Lake Tahoe ski resorts) that runs through the center of the building and stretches a quarter-mile or so up the hillside to several dig sites. The tram's thick support cable, while well-rusted after decades of neglect, still looks like it could haul a fair bit of ore.

If you walk alongside the tram, up the hill, you can get a great view of the mill and surrounding area. Nearby are several of the area's once-lucrative mines, which included such colorfully named shafts as the Dog Star, Jenny A. and Mary Ellen. Again, be cautious about exploring the area because mine shafts are dangerous.

To the rear of the mill are rusted ore cart rails which lead to an area where the processed ore was dumped into cargo containers and transported to a refinery.

Adjacent to the large mill structure are other metal buildings, including the original office, as well as a boarding house (still boasting metal bed frames) and a machine shop, which contains some larger tools and assorted pieces of equipment.

All of the buildings are posted with signs proclaiming they are federal government property and warning visitors not to touch or remove anything under penalty of law.

While a business district never developed at Belmont Mill, there are also a handful of decaying wooden structures on a hill above the mill, which appear to have been residences. Below the abandoned row of houses you'll also find several rusted hulks of cars of more recent vintage.

Belmont Mill, which records indicate was built by the Tonopah-Belmont Development Company of nearby Nye County, was active for only about ten years and didn't produce much ore of value. Despite its relatively short life, the mill is a classic example of a turn-of-the-century Nevada mining camp and has undoubtedly survived better than most. ❧

Candelaria

Fading Candelaria

THE SCENE IS A BIT INCONGRUOUS; in the foreground are the picturesque stone ruins of a bank, its front arched windows still guarded by rusted shutters, while in the distance massive trucks rumble up a gravel road leading to a large open pit mine.

Candelaria is an example of the old and new aspects of Nevada mining. The handful of stone and wooden remains represent the past, while the trucks, sprawling leaching ponds and tall cyclone fences tell the story of more modern mining in the state.

Due to neglect and abuse, Candelaria is gradually losing its battle to survive. Once the largest community in this section of central Nevada, Candelaria is slowly being reclaimed by the desert. Indeed, photos of Candelaria taken twenty-five years ago show many of the same buildings, but in much better shape and in greater number.

The best remains include the former bank building, which, according to records, later served as a saloon and general store, a second fairly intact stone building across the street as well as a handful of stone foundations, wooden walls, fences and collapsed ruins.

The two stone structures are the most substantial survivors of a main street that once stretched for about a half-mile or so through this small, dry valley surrounded by rough, black lava-rock hills.

Candelaria sits 14 miles south of Mina, off U.S. Highway 95 via a marked, paved road (which leads to the modern mining operation). Mina is located about 35 miles south of Hawthorne in central western Nevada.

History indicates silver was first discovered in Candelaria in the early 1860s by roaming Spanish prospectors. The name, Candelaria, which means "Candle Mass," a former Catholic holiday, was apparently derived from a mine of that name that was staked in 1864.

Large scale mining, however, did not begin until the mid-1870s, with development of the lucrative "Northern Belle" mine. Within a few years, large stamp mills were erected at nearby Belleville (eight miles northwest) and a typical western mining boom was under way.

In 1876, a visitor to Candelaria could find a post office, hotels, restaurants, stables and a budding business district. Water, however, was scarce and expensive, costing as much as $1 per gallon (it cost $2 to bathe!).

By the early 1880s, the mines were producing more than $1 million a year and the town had arrived. A water pipeline was built in 1882 from nearby Trail Canyon and the price of the precious commodity dipped to five cents per gallon.

Candelaria, by then, had a population of more than 1,500 (who presumably were bathing more often), making it the largest city in the county. The town had three doctors, two lawyers, a school, bank, telegraph office, two breweries, a newspaper and two dozen saloons — but, despite its Christian name, no churches (in fact, the town never had a church).

Another important event for the town also happened in 1882 with completion of a spur of the Carson & Colorado Railroad. The route connected Candelaria to shipping points at Mina and Keeler, a town near Owens Lake, California.

As with many 19th century Nevada mining towns, a fire destroyed part of the budding metropolis in 1883. The next year, a strike at the mines affected the area's output. That was followed by a gradual decline of the mines.

By 1890, the town had begun its descent into obscurity, reviving briefly just after the turn of the century with new mining discoveries. The railroad finally abandoned the area in 1932 (having been consolidated with other railroad lines in 1905 to become the Nevada & California Railway), after providing only intermittant service during the previous three decades.

The modern open pit gold mining operations were initiated about a decade ago, which obliterated much of the area around the historic mining district and overwhelmed the once peaceful valley. Large chain-link fences surround the new mine, which overlooks the old town. ❧

Hamilton

Hamilton is Ghost
of Itself

CRICKETS CHIRPING IN THE TALL GRASS that surrounds the weathered remains of a half-dozen brick and wooden buildings are the only permanent residents of the mining town of Hamilton in eastern Nevada.

Once the largest city in White Pine County, with more than 4,000 inhabitants (although a historic marker claims as many as 10,000), Hamilton will soon be little more than an historical footnote. The familiar combination of abandonment, the elements, theft and vandalism have just about assured that Hamilton probably will not survive for the next generation.

In the meantime, visitors can still gingerly wander through the handful of crumbling buildings that are littered about in the shadow of White Pine Mountain, adjacent to the once appropriately-named Treasure Hill.

Hamilton is located 12 miles south of Highway 50 at a point about 35 miles west of Ely. To reach the townsite, follow the signs from the highway on a well-maintained dirt road.

187

Two of Hamilton's ruins provide some idea of the significance of the town. The tallest is the sandstone, red brick and wooden structure that was once the two-story Withington Hotel.

Studying the ruins, it's easy to see that it was an impressive building with several chimneys, suggesting a luxury hard to imagine in such a remote and harsh environment.

A couple of hundred yards away, you can find the arched brick facade of what was once the Wells Fargo building. This leaning wall of molded red clay blocks somehow held together by scraps of wood and mortar likewise hints at a surprising quality of workmanship.

Exploring the scattered mounds of sagebrush and rubble, you can find foundations, stone walls and wooden studs of other buildings. They are spread across a fairly large area, providing an idea of the size of this town, which was also the original seat of White Pine County.

Surrounding the remains, visitors will find the evidence of more modern mining operations, including several rusted trailers on a hillside above the townsite, large metal buildings, pieces of equipment and the recognizable shallow pool of an abandoned leaching pond.

Hamilton's mineral reserves were first discovered in 1865 by a group of prospectors from Austin, Nevada. Their diggings identified several elements, including copper, lead, silver and iron, and the White Pine Mining District was formed.

By 1868, larger silver deposits had been found around Treasure Hill, sparking one of the most intense silver rushes in the state's history. A city was incorporated and named for promoter W.H. Hamilton the following year.

For a handful of years, Hamilton was the center of an incredible level of activity as other mining towns cropped up in the district, including places called Shermantown, Eberhardt and Treasure City.

Despite the fact that a fine brick courthouse was constructed in Hamilton in 1870, the boom proved shortlived. The silver turned out to be generously spread across the surface but maddeningly shallow. By 1871, the town had begun a rapid decline.

Two years later, a local merchant torched many of the town's buildings, hoping to collect some insurance and assuring the end of White Pine County's first city. By 1875, the town had been disincorporated and in 1885, the courthouse burned to the ground.

Not too many cared when the county seat was moved to Ely later that year.

Unfortunately, Hamilton's relative accessibility to Highway 50 has contributed to its disappearance. Local residents tell of ghost town explorers and bottle hunters who literally looted it out of existence during the 1950s.

For more information, contact the White Pine Chamber of Commerce, (702) 289-8877. ❧

Ione

Ione Gets Respect

THE HISTORIC COMMUNITY OF IONE might best be termed the "Rodney Dangerfield" of Nevada mining camps — a place that hasn't received much respect over the years, but has somehow managed to survive.

To reach Ione, travel east on Highway 50 to Middle Gate (about 40 miles east of Fallon). Turn south on State Route 361 toward Gabbs. Just before reaching Gabbs, turn east on State Route 91 (marked for the Berlin-Ichthyosaur State Park). Continue for about 12 miles, then turn north on the dirt road marked for Ione, before reaching Berlin-Ichthyosaur.

Originally settled in 1864, Ione is one of the oldest towns in the state. History books reveal that silver was first discovered in the Ione Valley a year earlier and a town called Ione City quickly developed, which served as the first county seat of newly created Nye County.

About 600 people settled in the prosperous little community.

However, by 1865, the more lucrative mineral finds at Belmont attracted most of Ione's citizens away — as well as the county seat, which moved to Belmont in 1867.

Modest silver discoveries in 1868 would normally have guaranteed Ione's success, but the larger White Pine mining boom of the same year attracted more attention and Ione never achieved its previous stature.

Ione's initial boom had ended by 1880, but the town managed to hang on, never being completely abandoned and subject to recurrent activity. In the 1920s and 1930s, mercury mining provided some sustenance to the area.

The town's real revival occurred in 1983, with the development of a large, modern gold mining operation by Marshall Earth Resources, Inc. In the mid-1980s, the mining company, which owns most of the town, set about restoring several of the original buildings.

In the course of a few years, the old schoolhouse was converted into a general store, while the post office was turned into the offices of Marshall Earth Resources (and furnished with some lovely antiques and furniture).

Another special treat is the Victorian-style town park in the center of the small hamlet. Encircled with a white picket fence, boasting old London-style street lamps and shaded by large trees, the park is a pleasant place for a picnic or to stop and enjoy the quiet surroundings.

Additionally, Ione's main center of business and commerce is the Ore House Saloon, a restaurant and bar, with a lot of rustic atmosphere, that serves pretty good burgers and fries.

If you wander around Ione, you'll also find some other interesting sights, including, just north of the general store, a corral filled with a half-dozen buffalo. A sign warns you not to get too close to these giant, woolly animals, who are known to be less than friendly.

North of the town park, you will find other remnants from the original Ione such as an aged, wooden corral fence, an old wooden building with classic frontier facade (rumored to have once served as a courthouse) and several rude, half-buried dirt and grass structures that may once have been miner's residences.

The nearby Ione Valley is also notable because historic evidence indicates it once boasted a large, permanent native American population, dating back more than 5,000 years.

Ione is located on the edge of the beautiful and majestic Toiyabe Mountain Range. A gravel road northeast of Ione heads into the northern part of the range, then passes over the Ione Summit, before dropping down into the Reese River Valley. From here, it is about 40 miles to Highway 50 and the town of Austin.

For more information about Ione, contact the Berlin-Ichthyosaur State Park, c/o the Nevada Division of State Parks, Capitol Complex, Carson City, NV 89710, (702) 687-4387. ❧

Kingston

Spectacular
Kingston Canyon

On SOME ROAD MAPS, central Nevada seems to consist of the town of Austin and lots of empty basin and range land. But hidden in the canyons, mountains and valleys, explorers will find dozens of historic sites and natural attractions that make a drive through the region worthwhile.

One of the most beautiful of central Nevada's lesser known scenic gems is Kingston Canyon, which is featured in an excellent new free brochure, called "Central Nevada Driving Tours."

Kingston Canyon is located 27 miles southeast of Austin. To reach the area, travel 17 miles east on U.S. Highway 50 to State Route 376, then head south for about four miles to Kingston Creek Road, which leads into the canyon.

At the mouth of Kingston Canyon, you'll pass through a relatively developed area consisting of about a dozen ranch homes and a few larger buildings, including a general store and church. Just past the new development, to the right, you'll spot the last remnants of Kingston, a mid-19th century mining camp.

Perhaps the best ruin is the former Victorine Mill, which consists of fairly substantial stone walls and large timbers. Around the mill site, there are also the scattered foundations and walls of other structures no longer identifiable.

From here, you can start driving up on a maintained dirt road into Kingston Canyon. The canyon walls offer some impressive rock formations and classic Nevada pinion and sagebrush landscape.

The road rises above the surrounding Big Smoky Valley — offering a wonderful view — into the Toiyabe Range. About a mile from the canyon entrance, you reach the rustic Kingston Forest Campgrounds, operated by the National Forest Service.

A bit farther is a pretty, small reservoir, a popular local fishing spot. From here, the road curves around Bunker Hill (the 11,474-foot-high peak to the north) and rides the crest of the Toiyabe range for a few miles, paralleling Kingston Creek.

The scenery here is incredible; to the west you can see the beauty of the Reese River Valley, while to the east is the spectacular Big Smoky. A few miles ahead, Kingston Creek becomes Big Creek and the road reaches the Big Creek Forest Campground, a relatively undeveloped back country campsite.

The road continues northwest from the campground, dropping down into the Reese River Valley at a point about ten miles south of Highway 50 and Austin.

Records indicate that silver and gold were discovered in the Kingston area in the early 1860s. A small camp, originally called Bunker Hill, was established and existed for about two years.

In 1864, Kingston was staked near the entrance of the canyon to be closer to the mines. Several mills were built, including the massive Victorine, and, because of the availability of water from the creek, a number of crops were planted, including grapes (which apparently did not flourish).

By the end of the decade, it became obvious that the Kingston ore wasn't as rich as originally believed and the town began to decline. The mills were dismantled and moved to other locations.

Kingston's mines were reworked several times in later years, including in the 1880s and at the turn-of-the-century. Today, the area remains a sleepy ranching hamlet with occasional activity at the Kingston Lodge, a local restaurant.

For more information and a copy of the new "Central Nevada Driving Tours" brochure (which also features information on driving to Toquima Cave, Diana's Punchbowl and other fascinating central Nevada attractions), contact the Austin Chamber of Commerce, Box 212, Austin, NV 89310, (702) 964-2200. ✒

Manhattan

This
Manhattan
is No Big Apple

IT WAS GOLD AND SILVER, not a couple of bucks in beads and necklaces, that created Nevada's Manhattan.

But unlike its more well known eastern namesake, Nevada's Manhattan never quite developed into a famous metropolitan center. Instead, the Silver State's Manhattan, like all mining towns, has had a roller coaster existence, its fortunes paralleling the condition of its mining industry.

Manhattan is located about 45 miles north of Tonopah via State Routes 376 and 377.

Today, visitors will find that despite neglect and the virtual obliteration of much of its original mining district by modern open pit gold mining operations, Manhattan has a handful of historic buildings and sites worth visiting.

Perhaps the best of Manhattan's hearty survivors is the picturesque frontier-style wooden Manhattan Catholic Church, sitting on a hillside overlooking the town.

Built in 1874 in nearby Belmont, the classic old west church was abandoned by 1901, then moved to Manhattan in 1908. In the 1970s, a handful of local residents restored the church, which remains popular for wedding ceremonies.

The hillsides surrounding the town are dotted with the hulking skeletons of old mining headframes. The town's main street is lined with a handful of historic buildings, including several rustic saloons, still operating, and a few turn-of-the-century homes. In the center of the community is the old bank building with its vault intact (although, alas, it's empty inside — I looked!).

Additionally, the locals do conduct a rather unique sporting event during the town's Founder's Day celebration each summer. Called the "chicken hit contest," it involves putting a chicken inside a square, fenced arena, about eight foot by eight foot, that has a wooden floor painted with a grid of numbers inside squares. Participants bet on which number the chicken will "hit" when he relieves himself. Honest.

Perhaps the most historic building in the town is the John C. Humphrey home, a small green and white cottage with Victorian architecture. Humphrey was one of the founders of modern Manhattan and the man who rediscovered silver at the site. His descendents still own the house.

History books indicate that silver was first discovered in the area in 1866 by a man named George Nicholl. Within a short time, more than fifty mines were operating in the region, which became known as Manhattan Gulch.

But by 1869, the district seemed tapped out and activity ceased. The area remained dormant until 1905, when Humphrey, a cowboy from the nearby Big Smoky Valley, stumbled onto an outcropping while searching for cattle.

Samples removed by Humphrey and three friends were tested, proving to be rich in silver ore and Manhattan's revival was under way. The town was erected almost overnight and within a few months had a post office, saloons, hotels, schools, telephone and telegraph service, three banks and two newspapers.

As with many early 20th century mining camps, the San Francisco earthquake in 1906 severely affected investment in Manhattan and signaled the beginning of the end of the town's second boom.

The population plummeted from a high of 4,000 people to a few hundred, who scrambled to survive with new discoveries. The discovery of large gold reserves in 1909, however, again revived the town.

The town prospered into the 1920s, then declined once more. In 1939, a 3000 ton gold dredge was built below the town in the Manhattan Gulch (site of the original silver discovery). The operation, which included a large pond created from water piped from nearby Peavine Creek, flourished until 1946 when the dredge was removed.

In 1979, a massive open pit heap-leaching operation was started there by Houston International Minerals Company.

For more information, contact the Tonopah Chamber of Commerce, Box 869, Tonopah, NV 89049, (702) 482-3558. ❧

Marietta

Borax Legend
Started in
Marietta

A DRY WIND SWEEPS ACROSS a powdery alkali lake bed and gently blows through the tufts of sagebrush growing around the handful of stone walls and foundations that are all that remains of the town of Marietta.

Marietta is located 56 miles southwest of Hawthorne via U.S. Highway 95, then west on State Route 360 to a marked and well-maintained dirt road.

Founded in the late 1870s, Marietta was not a typical central Nevada mining camp because its fortunes were not based on gold and silver, but on borax and salt.

Originally known as Teels Marsh, the area was first developed in 1867 when salt was mined in the flat and transported by camel train to Virginia City's booming mines (salt was used in the processing of the ore).

In 1872, Francis M. Smith, who would later become renowned as "Borax" Smith, was working the salt fields in nearby Columbus and spotted the borate potential of the marsh. He and his brother took samples from the dry lake bed, which proved to be rich in borax, and staked much of the area.

Full scale borax mining begin within months of the discovery as the Smiths and other miners began constructing borax plants at the southeastern end of the marsh. Records indicate that wagon trains hauled the material all the way to the train station at Wadsworth, about 115 miles north.

The Teels Marsh borax field was not only an important discovery for Nevada, but, as a result, the Smiths created the Teel's Marsh Borax Company. This was the precursor to the Pacific Borax Salt & Soda Co., which would eventually control the world borax market.

Smith's genius was that he recognized the value of borax if marketed correctly. Prior to his efforts, borax was used primarily in pharmaceuticals and mined only in Europe.

Since he was sitting on such large reserves, Smith began promoting and advertising the substance as an effective abrasive cleaner. He created an immense market for his products and, in the process, became one of the early 20th century's most successful industrialists.

Smith would eventually move farther west to larger borax (colmanite) discoveries in Death Valley and become famed for his 40-mule teams that carried the ore out of the Death Valley area (another example of his advertising acumen).

The town of Marietta wasn't started until 1877 and, within a year, had a post office, a newspaper, a company store owned by Borax Smith, several other businesses and more than 150 residents. A stamp mill was erected in the first year to help in the ore processing.

Within a few years, the town had a row of buildings, including a dozen saloons on its main street as well as the large stamp mill and several dozen wooden and rock houses.

The discovery of the richer borax deposits at Death Valley eventually signaled the end of Marietta. By the 1890s, the borax operations were abandoned and the town began its rapid slide into oblivion.

The drive to Marietta is an opportunity to view the real Nevada outback. The road winds through rolling sage-covered foothills before dropping down into the flat, treeless, alkali valley that is the location of Teels Marsh and, at the southeast end of the marsh, the ruins of Marietta.

The town's signature structure is the stone wall remains of the Smith store. You can still find three of the four walls of the store standing, with a second structure, perhaps a later addition, directly east of the walls.

Just east of the store are the foundations and remains of the mill and, buried in the sagebrush, a handful of neglected, rude mounds can be found in the original cemetary.

Additionally, near the main street there are a handful of wooden farmhouses, including one with a fairly intact stone corral and walls that appeared to have been insulated with old cardboard Crisco boxes. Another small, one-story wooden structure with a frontier storefront and a decided tilt, is still identified as the post office.

A few mobile homes and ranch houses surround the ruins and indicate that Marietta can still claim a few residents.

More recently, the area around Teels Marsh and Marietta has been designated as the nation's first formally recognized wild burro range. The 68,000-acre range is home to about 85 burros that can freely roam the marsh and surrounding hills.

The range, created this year, is a refuge for the burros and one of the few places the public is invited to view the wild burros (although you aren't supposed to feed or touch them). There are designated viewing areas above the marsh.

Visitors will also find, just across the dirt road leading to Marietta, the nearly unrecognizable remains of Belleville (an historic marker indicates the location), another central Nevada mining camp. The ghost town of Candelaria is located about 15 miles south of Marietta via a marked dirt road about a mile west of the turn-off to Marietta. ❧

Metropolis

Fate Not Kind
to Cursed
Metropolis

METROPOLIS NEVER REALLY HAD MUCH of a chance to succeed.

In 1909, a New York land development company, Pacific Reclamation Company, decided that northwestern Nevada was the perfect locale for developing a new town.

Pacific Reclamation's plans called for a modern city with a population of 7,500, surrounded by more than 40,000 acres of cultivated agricultural land. A dam would be built at the confluence of three streams that fed the Humboldt River to provide water for the community.

The company opened an office in Salt Lake City to sell lots on the site. By 1911, streets, parcels and a pair of parks were drawn up on maps and a twice-monthly newspaper was started.

A four-block business district began to take shape with construction of a $100,000 high-rise brick hotel, a post office, a half-dozen saloons and a handful of other commercial enterprises. The Southern Pacific Railroad also built an eight mile spur from its main line and erected a depot with a park and water fountain.

In 1912, work was completed on a 100 foot dam, a series of canals and an elaborate water system designed to provide water for the new paradise, which was given the rather optimistic name, Metropolis.

Records indicate that by the next year, more than 700 people, most of whom were members of the Mormon Church, had purchased land and moved into the new town. Additionally, work began on a beautiful red brick school building and there was serious talk of moving the county seat from Elko to Metropolis.

Metropolis' bright future, however, proved illusory. In the first place, the land developers promoted an agricultural wonderland in an area with perhaps one of the shortest growing seasons in the country.

More importantly, however, in 1913, farmers from the Lovelock region filed a lawsuit against Pacific Reclamation claiming that it had no rights to the water in streams it had dammed. The courts sided with the upstream users and declared that Metropolis was entitled to water from only one of the creeks — enough water to irrigate 4,000 acres — far less than planned.

At the same time, the region entered a multi-year drought — not unlike recent conditions in Nevada — and crops began to shrivel and die.

In late 1913, Pacific Reclamation filed for bankruptcy protection. Despite that, the community continued to struggle on, completing the school in 1914. While most residents moved away during the next few years, the farmers that remained did find they had enough water to successfully raise wheat and potatoes.

Dairy farming also took hold in 1917 and by the early 1920s, Metropolis was shipping cream by railroad to a dairy in Reno.

But Metropolis proved to be a cursed town. Hordes of jack rabbits invaded the area, destroying most crops. That was followed by a six year invasion by swarms of giant Mormon crickets who also ate just about everything they could find.

By 1925, the end of Metropolis seemed inevitable. The Southern Pacific removed its track and the remaining buildings that could be moved were sold and relocated. The huge hotel burned down in 1936, the post office was closed in 1942 and the school was abandoned in 1947.

Today, Metropolis remains not only an interesting historic anecdote, but an intriguing place to visit. The site of Metropolis is located 14 miles northwest of Wells via a paved and signed road (making it one of the most accessible of Nevada's ghost towns).

A handful of remains stand in silent tribute to the dreams of those who attempted to create a paradise out of the sagebrush and cheat grass. The ruins seem out of place — huge Stonehenges surrounded by the same sage and grass in the middle of a serene, seemingly untouched valley.

Most impressive is the solitary stone arch of the old school. The rest of the brick building has disintegrated (or been removed), but the intricate design of the arch illustrates the care and work that went into the construction of Metropolis.

A quarter-mile away are the ruins of the hotel, now almost completely reclaimed by the sagebrush. A cemetary and other foundations can also be found in the area. A few miles away, via dirt roads, you can also still find the dam that provided water to Metropolis.

A maintained stone monument tells the story of Metropolis and is dedicated to the hard-working people who were perhaps the first victims of the kind of land speculation that has also become a part of Nevada's history.

For information about Metropolis, contact the Wells Chamber of Commerce, Box 615, Wells, NV 89835, (702) 752-3540. An informative video about Metropolis and the Wells area, prepared by the Northeastern Nevada Museum, can be purchased at the Burger Bar Restaurant in Wells, 752-3210. ❧

Pine Grove

Forgotten
Pine Grove

IT DOESN'T SHOW UP on too many Nevada road maps, but the ghost town of Pine Grove is one of the better preserved and accessible of the state's historic mining camps.

Pine Grove is located about 26 miles south of Yerington. To reach it, head 11 miles south on State Route 208, then turn onto an unmarked but well maintained dirt road. Follow the dirt road for 11 miles, then turn right on Pine Grove Mine Road (it's marked). Continue west for four miles to the remains of Pine Grove.

The town is located in Pine Grove Canyon, a heavily wooded, ruggedly beautiful slash in the eastern slopes of the Pine Grove Hills. The journey up into the canyon passes through scenic, craggy cliffs and gullies.

Gold was originally discovered in the canyon in 1866 by William Wilson. A second mine, called the Wheeler Mine, was started soon after and within two years there were two large mills in operation, a post office, a weekly newspaper and a population of about 300.

Additionally, a stage and freight line was established, which connected the mining camp to nearby Wellington in the Smith Valley. By the early 1870s, the town claimed some 600 people and a variety of businesses, ranging from saloons and hotels to a school and blacksmith shop.

By 1893, the Wilson mine had produced more than $5 million, while the Wheeler generated some $3 million, both largely in gold ore with traces of silver. The mines began to decline just before that time although there was activity in 1900 and again in 1910.

While smaller mining operators continued to work the old tailing piles for a number of years, most significant activity ended by 1918. The dirt road leading to the town was built in 1904 during one of the later mining revivals.

Today, Pine Grove is only a shadow of its former glory, but still claims enough to make it interesting. At the east end of the town, visitors will find an informative historic marker adjacent to the stone remains of a former building.

A little farther up the canyon you can find the remains of a leaching operation from the 1960s. Fortunately, the more modern mining work did not destroy a fine wooden and rusted iron stamp mill, still standing on a hill, or the horizontal mining shafts that reach deep into the mountainside.

One hole was particularly interesting because of an intricate stone wall that had been constructed near the entrance (perhaps once part of a building at the opening of the mine).

Of course, as with any abandoned shaft, it's safe to look at from a distance, but never enter the mine. Additionally, the shafts and stamp mill are located on marked, private property.

About a quarter-of-a-mile from the mining area are the best remains of Pine Grove. Here, you will still find two fairly-well preserved wooden structures, one apparently an old boarding house or hotel, while the other appears to have been a garage or storage building. Again, look, but don't touch.

If you wander through the high sagebrush around the town's remains, it's also still possible to find the remnants of other buildings, such as partial walls and stone foundations.

Directly east of the center of the former town, you'll also pass the ruins of a more recent placer operation (they appear to be from the 1960s mining efforts). Here, the rusting remains of various mechanical processing machines have become the newest ghostly remains at Pine Grove.

A good map of the Pine Grove area can be found in the Nevada Map Atlas, produced by the Nevada Department of Transportation. For more information, contact NDOT, Map Section, Room 206, 1263 South Stewart St., Carson City, NV 89712, (702) 687-3451. ❧

Rhyolite

Rhyolite
Recalls Nevada's
Mining Past

THE DESERT HAS NOT BEEN KIND TO RHYOLITE. Once impressive concrete, stone and brick buildings have been blasted by wind and sand into skeletal reminders of a place that was one of Nevada's most promising mining towns.

Sitting on the edge of Nevada, overlooking Death Valley, Rhyolite more than almost any other ghost town tells the story of the rise and fall of a Nevada mining town.

Rhyolite is located about four miles west of Beatty, via State Route 374 and U.S. Highway 95.

Gold was discovered here in 1904 and a township was mapped during the following year. In May, 1905, the town had its own newspaper, showing that it had come of age.

A month later, a post office was opened and by 1907, an estimated 6,000 people had flocked to this boom town in the desert.

Soon, no less than three railroads (the Las Vegas and Tonopah, Tonopah and Tidewater and Bullfrog-Goldfield) were built to serve the town along with 45 saloons, an opera house, a telephone company, electric power plant, three ice plants, several hotels and two stock exchanges.

Major buildings were constructed to serve the growing population. Photographs show at least a handful of multiple-story concrete buildings, including the J.S. Cook bank building, the school house and the Overbury bank building.

Rhyolite benefited from the success of Nevada's other early 20th century mining towns, Tonopah and Goldfield. Much of the money used to build the town was invested by those who missed out on the earlier booms and hoped to experience similiar results.

Unfortunately, many of those selling shares in mines were unscrupulous speculators. Additionally, Rhyolite turned out to be a bit of a disappointment in terms of gold production. While there was gold in the area, it wasn't in sufficient quantities and accessible enough to justify the development that had appeared almost overnight.

Another problem was the 1906 San Francisco earthquake. Many of Rhyolite's investors lived in San Francisco and, following the earthquake, were more interested in rebuilding their lives than spending money on a questionable investment in Nevada.

The final blow was a national financial panic in 1907. As a result, the money began to dry up for developing Rhyolite's mines and people began to move on to more profitable places. In 1910, the street lights were turned off and the water company announced it could no longer service the community.

The remaining newspaper, The Rhyolite Herald (there were three at the town's peak), chronicled the decline until 1911, when even it could not continue.

The Herald's stories during the latter half of 1910 report a community-wide firesale — on May 7, the Porter store sold its entire stock; on May 28, the Commercial Hotel was sold, with the building and furniture moved to Las Vegas; and on December 31, the bank's vault doors, deposit boxes, furniture and fixtures were sold for one-sixth the original costs.

The census of 1910 indicated 675 residents and a decade later the number was fourteen.

Today, Rhyolite remains one of the most photogenic of Nevada's ghost towns. In the late afternoon, the sun stretches the shadows of the ruins, creating marvelous images.

The town contains some intriguing structures, including the three-story exterior walls of the Cook bank building, the facade of the Porter brothers store and the interesting remains of the school building.

The former Las Vegas and Tonopah Railroad depot is one of the finest examples of the early 20th century mission-style architecture used for many public buildings.

Rhyolite is also home of one of the last mostly-intact bottle houses in the state. Constructed using more than 50,000 bottles (at a time when building materials were scarce), the home has been allowed to decline in recent years. There's a fence around it, as well as the depot, to protect the buildings.

Adjacent to the ghost town is a major modern open pit mining operation — proving that Rhyolite was just a little bit ahead of its time.

For more information, contact the Beatty Chamber of Commerce, P.O. Box 956, Beatty, NV 89003, (702) 553-2424. ❧

PART VI

Other Stuff

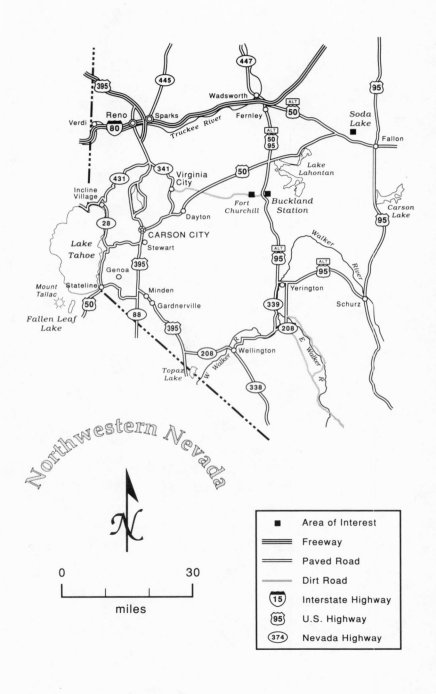

Northwestern Nevada

N

0   30

miles

■   Area of Interest
═══ Freeway
─── Paved Road
╌╌╌ Dirt Road
(15) Interstate Highway
(95) U.S. Highway
(374) Nevada Highway

Other Stuff

IN BOTH "BACKYARD TRAVELER" BOOKS, I have attempted to follow some kind of general geographic outline in presenting the material. But since I continue to write "Backyard Traveler" columns every week, there are a few places I would have included in the first book, except for the fact I'd not written about them when that book was compiled. Those are the "Other Stuff."

The following featured places are all located in the northern part of the state (which really messes up the subtitle to this book). But, for a variety of reasons, I feel strongly about each and would like to share my observations with you.

Included are stories about the historic Stewart Indian Museum, one of the few places to spotlight Nevada's rich Native American history, culture and art, as well as the haunting remains of American Flats, another of the reminders of the glory that was the Comstock Lode.

Additionally, I've written about the unusual Basque carvings found on a grove of aspens above Glenbrook, the simple beauty of the Pony Express road to Fort Churchill, the incredible majesty of Fallen Leaf Lake and the splendor of Lake Tahoe's Tallac Historic Site, once home to an earlier generation of America's rich and famous.

A story I couldn't overlook is the one about Bob Gray's herculean efforts to rebuild the Virginia and Truckee Railroad line from Virginia City to Gold Hill. We can only hope he someday realizes his goal of extending the line all the way to Carson City.

Lastly, I couldn't omit one of my favorite stories — an overview of some of the better books written about Nevada. As a devoted book collector and Nevadaphile, I've accumulated a small collection of books about the state, many of which make wonderful reading as well as excellent gifts. Not surprisingly, this column originally appeared in slightly different form just before Christmas.

Nevada's Native American Repository

NEVADA'S NATIVE AMERICANS have a rich history and culture. One of the best places to learn more about the state's original people is Carson City's Stewart Indian Museum.

The Stewart Indian Museum and Trading Post is located at 5366 Snyder Avenue, at the south end of Carson City.

The museum, which sits on the grounds of the former Stewart Indian Boarding School, was founded in 1982 to tell the story of the boarding school as well as celebrate the history, arts, crafts and traditions of Native American people.

The first thing a visitor notices about the museum and surrounding buildings is the unique architecture. Built with walls of rough-cut, multi-colored native stones imbedded in dark mortar, the buildings have a kind of "homemade" feel.

According to historical reports, the so-called "Stewart Indian School" architecture was a style borrowed in the early 1920s by then-superintendent Frederick Snyder, who had admired a church of similar design in Arizona.

The first building of this design (the former Administrative Building, which is still standing directly east of the museum) was completed in 1923. Eventually more than 100 buildings utilizing the stone architecture were constructed on the school grounds, most built by stone masons trained at the school.

Inside the museum building, which was originally the Superintendent's Cottage, you can find a series of photos and displays describing the school's 90-year history. Additionally, there are several rooms and galleries displaying historic artifacts as well as contemporary Native American art.

For example, the main art gallery features works of well known native artists such as Ben Aleck, Dugan Aguilar, Jean LaMar, Jack Malotte and Lucinda Benjamin.

One hallway contains a fine collection of the historical photos of E.J. Curtis, an early 20th century photographer who presented Native Americans in somewhat romanticized scenes of Indian life.

One of the display rooms has a nice collection of Washo, Paiute and Shoshone baskets and cradleboards as well as an interesting bronze sculpture of famed Washo basket-maker, Dat-So-La-Lee, by Bill Shaffer.

A well-stocked trading post in the center of the building offers a wide selection of Indian jewelry, art, books and traditional crafts that are for sale.

The Stewart Indian School story began in the 1880s when Nevada's Superintendent of Public Instruction, C.S. Young, recommended to the U.S. Bureau of Indian Affairs and the Nevada State Legislature that an Indian industrial school be established because most of the state's Native Americans were not being formally educated.

The Nevada State Legislature passed legislation in 1887 that established an Indian school and authorized the issuing of bonds for the facility, provided the federal government agreed to operate the school.

Nevada's U.S. Senator William Stewart guided the appropriate federal legislation to approval, including congressional funding, and the Clear Creek Indian Training School, as it was originally known, was built by the Bureau of Indian Affairs on 240 acres.

Later, the school was named for Senator Stewart (it was called a number of names over the years, including the Carson Indian School, the Stewart Institute and, finally, the Stewart Indian School) and officially opened on December 17, 1890.

Records indicate that on opening day, the school had a superintendent (W.D.C. Gibson), three teachers and 37 students from the Paiute, Washo and Shoshone tribes. Within a month, additional students were added, bringing the co-educational enrollment to 91 by January 1, 1891.

The school was operated much like a military school in its first decades. Historic photos show that students wore military-style uniforms. Academic classes consumed about half of each day, followed by vocational training in such skills as sewing, shoe and harness-making, black-smithing, carpentry, printing and other work.

The museum's "Hall of Fame" room spotlights two of the areas for which Stewart's students gained some measure of fame: athletics and music.

Beginning in the 1890s, the Stewart athletic teams played a variety of sports, including football, track, basketball, boxing and baseball. While relatively small in size, the school still managed to win several state championships, including a 1916 state football title, seven consecutive state "AA" cross country championships in the 1970s and the 1966 state "A" basketball championship.

Over the years, the school's award-winning band, organized in 1896, performed at parades and events throughout the state and in other competition, including a National Music Festival in Long Beach, California, in 1940.

The school was also responsible for producing Nevada's first Native American newspaper, "The Indian Advance," which was published in 1899. Samples of several historic early 20th century native publications are on display in the museum.

In addition to educating Nevada's Native Americans (who were actually a minority of those who ever attended the school), the Stewart facility housed Native Americans from throughout the country. In fact, in the late 1940s, the school became part of a special program for Navajos and by the mid-50s, most of the students were of Navajo descent.

The school was finally closed in 1980, after the federal government decided to phase out many of its Indian boarding schools. The land was sold to the state of Nevada, which deeded three of the buildings to the non-profit Stewart Indian Museum.

The museum is open daily (excluding Christmas), from 9 a.m. to 4 p.m. For more information, contact the Stewart Indian Museum, (702) 882-1808. ෴

Stewart Indian Museum

Sad, Ghostly Remains
of
American Flat

NEVADA SOMETIMES DOESN'T TREAT its historic sites particularly well and nowhere is that more apparent than at the ruins of American Flat.

Located just above Gold Hill in the Comstock region, American Flat (also known as American City) more resembles some post-World War III landscape from an end-of-the-world movie than the historic remains of what was once the nation's largest cyanide mill plant.

To reach American Flat travel 1 mile west of State Route 341 on a dirt road located directly across the highway from the road leading to the Cabin in the Sky restaurant. About halfway, either park and hike in the last half-mile or turn left on a rutted dirt road that leads down to the ruins.

Today, a visitor will find the huge remnants of the four-story cyanide plant and a vast labrynth of concrete foundations and ruins. The gray cement remains, however, have been covered with decades of cumulative graffitti — colorful and descriptive, but unfortunate.

Still, the site is a fascinating place to explore. The multi-story main building looks more like an abandoned parking garage and there are other strange and intriguing shapes in the twisted, hulking concrete ruins.

At the south end of the site, water still flows from some abandoned pipe system and trickles into a creek that passes down the hillside.

Standing under the graffitti-covered cement archways adjacent to the creek, there is a kind of disquiet and unease in the air — as if the site knows it deserves a better afterlife than the one it has been given.

Above the site is an apparently intermittent active mining operation, which is fenced and signed as private property.

The American Flat locale has also taken on a new role in recent years. Local war-gamers, utilizing guns that fire green and yellow "paint-balls" which simulate wounding a quarry — in a kind of elaborate game of tag — have adopted the ruins for their skirmishes.

During a recent visit, more than two dozen young men clad in fatigues with special goggles and masks to protect their heads were scurrying over the post-apocolypse ruins in mock combat. While they were well-behaved — even shouting, "civilians," whenever outsiders were in range — the scene was definitely bizarre.

Historic reports indicate that gold and silver were discovered at American Flat in the early 1860s. A town sprouted by 1864, as a kind of spillover from the intense mining activity occurring over the hill in Gold Canyon.

Interestingly, in 1864 the citizens of American Flat were sufficiently bullish on their community's future to attempt to wrestle away the territorial capital from Carson City. They offered $50,000 to state leaders if they would move the government to American Flat, but the proposal was rejected.

The town's initial incarnation was shortlived. Despite boasting a post office, a couple of hotels and other businesses, the town began to disintegrate in the late 1860s and was abandoned.

In 1920, the United Comstock Mining Company chose American Flat for the location of a $1.5 million cyanide plant to process ore from the nearby Comstock Lode, which was still being worked. A two mile railroad spur was built from the Virginia and Truckee Railroad line near Gold Hill.

Photos from the time show a 3000 ton mill that covered much of the hillside with acres of horizontal, multi-storied metal-sided buildings. A small hamlet developed north of the mill, in the area that is now part of the active mining operations on private property.

The expensive mill operated for about six years, then was closed for good when the price of silver dropped in the mid-1920s. The equipment and portions of the buildings were removed and sold, leaving behind the stark concrete skeletons found today.

For more information about American Flat, contact the Virginia City Chamber of Commerce, V&T Railroad Car, Virginia City, NV 89440, (702) 847-0311. ❧

American Flat

Basque Carvings

Ribald
Basque Carvings

OVERHEAD, THE BRIGHT SUN filters through the thin branches of hundreds of tall aspen trees, all clad in autumn yellow. A soft wind shakes the rounded leaves, causing a few more to join the crunchy carpet of fallen plant debris covering the ground.

Then I see what I'm looking for and begin to chuckle. It's a crude, stick-figure carving on one of the aspen of a man sitting before a piano on what appears to be a toilet seat. Carved above the foot-high image are the words: "E.M. 1932 . . . Playing the piano and —."

High above the east shore of Lake Tahoe, near Spooner Summit, is one of those unique places that make Nevada such a fascinating place to live. In this case, it's a grove of aspen trees in a high mountain meadow that once served as a summer range for Basque sheepherders and their flocks.

While not the only one found at the lake — in fact, aspen groves featuring Basque "graffiti" can be found in dozens of mountain ranges in the state — this particular place is one of the older and larger of these outdoor galleries.

The origin of these drawings has to do with the long stretches of time that Basqu sheepherders spent alone, tending their flocks.

To pass the time, many would carve initials, dates and other messages in the white bark of the aspen trees. Naturally, like spray-painted graffiti on a building wall in a large city, some of these doodlings would pertain to what was on the mind of the artist.

Wandering through the Spooner aspen grove (as I'll call this area), it's possible to find dozens of carvings. While a few are rather ribald — and reveal an excellent grasp of both male and female anatomy — others offer more intriguing information, such as initials and dates going back seventy and eighty years.

My particular favorite, apparently also carved by the multi-talented "E.M.," depicts a man riding on a horse. Dated August 21, 1932, the drawing is detailed enough to reveal the hat and scarf on the man as well as a saddle, whip and reins.

Another interesting carving shows a fairly detailed representation of the flag of Spain, with the words, "Espana, June 25, 1939," followed by words that are difficult to decipher (possibly Basque or Spanish words). Still others simply show carvings of men in striped shirts with cowboy hats.

After weaving for a time through the thickly wooded grove, it becomes apparent that the trees are a veritable white bark chalkboard of designs, words and drawings. In a few cases, the trees have become so old (aspen live to be about 90 years) that the bark has grown around the carvings, making them impossible to read.

The Spooner grove, like others in the Sierra Nevada, were part of a cycle common among those raising sheep in Nevada. In the winter, the sheep would be kept in the desert valleys, which were warmer and more habitable than the higher elevations.

However, in the summer months, the sheepherders would

move the flocks into the mountains to fatten on the thicker grasses found in the mountain meadows.

To reach the Spooner grove, travel west of Carson City on Highway 50. At the point where the road splits, heading north to Incline Village and south to Stateline, continue north for about a quarter-mile. Turn left just before the Spooner Summit Nevada Department of Transportation Maintenance Station and drive to the back of the facility.

There, you will find a paved road identified as Road 14N32. Follow the road for about three-quarters of a mile (it quickly becomes a dirt road). At that point, you reach a fork in the road and take the route to the right (you will pass a "1" painted on a tree about a fifth-of-a-mile from the fork).

From here, continue for about a mile, making sure you go left when you reach a second fork in the road (there are orange and black signs with arrows pointing to the left road).

About another quarter-of-a-mile from the second fork, you'll see a large lava rock formation to the right and the Spooner aspen grove on the left.

While the road is passable for vehicles with high clearance, a good way to visit is by hiking in the two miles from the maintenance station. While it is a steep climb, one has a greater sense of anticipation and accomplishment upon hiking to the grove — although I found myself greatly tempted to hitch a ride with one of the off-road vehicles or mountain bikers that pass on their way to the Lake Tahoe Rim Trail, located about a half-mile above the grove.

For more information, contact the U.S. Forest Service office, 1536 S. Carson Street, Carson City, (702) 882-2766. ❧

*Pony Express Route near
the Carson River*

Retracing
the
Pony Express

ONE OF THE MOST LASTING IMAGES of the Old West is the lone Pony Express rider racing across a stretch of open sage-covered landscape, uncertain of what lies ahead, but continuing because it's his job.

Despite the fact that the Pony Express only operated for about 18 months in 1860-61, the mythology of that uniquely American endeavor has captured our imaginations over the past 130 years.

While few of the original Pony Express station sites remain in Nevada — the best are at Sand Springs and Cold Springs, adjacent to modern U.S. Highway 50 — it is still possible to follow parts of the historic route, particularly since it passed right through our backyard.

A good place to retrace the old route is the road that parallels the Carson River, between Dayton and Fort Churchill.

The best way to join this road is to head east on Highway 50 to Dayton. About five miles from Dayton, turn right on a graded dirt road (it's marked Fort Churchill Road) that is opposite Six Mile Canyon Road.

Follow the road for about 1 mile, at which point you will reach another dirt road parallel to the Carson River. This is the former Pony Express route.

Except for the intrusion of power lines and barbed-wire fences, you can drive along this road — or better yet, walk or ride a horse — and see things pretty much as they were more than a century-and-a-quarter ago. Occasionally, you'll pass a small ranch or farm, but the route remains rugged, dusty and wild, as it must have been originally.

To your right, the river meanders along, lined with tall aspens, which will explode with color in the fall months. At several places along the road, you can find shaded areas on the river ideal for picnicking.

A few miles down the road, you reach fields of groomed, baled and stacked ha. At a place called the Chaves Ranch, there is evidence of a large cattle operation and a veritable museum of rusting farm machinery.

As if on cue, a woman driving a small green tractor pulls in front of me, then turns onto a side road and disappears almost as quickly,

Ahead, you can see Table Mountain, named because of its flat-top appearance. There is evidence of some kind of mining, now discontinued, on the west side of the mountain.

The road hugs the mountain as it squeezes between it and the river. Driving by the mountain, you can see small caves and dark recesses high in the beautiful, rocky cliff face.

A bit farther, you reach more buildings — again once part of a cattle operation — but now abandoned. The landscape opens wider here, with the river winding through large, grassy meadowlands.

About 12 miles since joining the road, the area suddenly

becomes developed with plenty of buildings and dozens of parked vehicles. A sign indicates that you have reached the Nevada Automotive Test Center, apparently a testing ground for a variety of transports.

It's a strange sight — all kinds of vehicles, ranging from mail trucks to military vehicles to buses to ambulences, parked behind high, wire fences. The complex includes several blacktop track areas as well as a railroad bed, complete with two train cars, but with no connecting tracks.

You wonder what the Pony Express rider would have made of it all.

From here, the land becomes more dry and barren, with only the river and its shrubbery providing any relief from the rolling hills of brown sagebrush and grass.

At about 14.5 miles, you finally spot the stark tan, clay remains of historic Fort Churchill, jutting out of the desert floor. Built in 1860 to protect settlers as well as the Pony Express riders, it must have been a welcome sight for them and marks the end of this particular stretch of the Pony Express route.

There are several good books on the Pony Express in Nevada, including a brief, but informative booklet from the Bureau of Land Management (Box 12000, Reno, NV 89520, (702) 785-6402). A lengthier version of this book was jointly published by BLM and Harrah's in 1976, to commemorate the Bicentennial, and can sometimes be found in used bookstores.

Additionally, a few years ago, Nevada historian John Townley wrote the excellent "Pony Express Guidebook," a detailed description of retracing the entire route across the state. The 60-page book is published by the Great Basin Studies Center, 7115 Pembroke Drive, Reno, NV 89502. ⁊

Buckland's Station

Historic
Stagecoach Stop

Iт's STILL POSSIBLE TO IMAGINE a creaking stagecoach led by two panting horses pulling up in front of old Buckland's Station to pick up the mail and deposit a few passengers.

Buckland's Station, located about 40 miles east of Carson City via Highway 50 and Alternate Highway 95, remains one of the few relatively intact Overland Stage stations in Nevada.

The large, two-story, faded-white wooden building, while not open to the public, is a fascinating reminder of an adventurous age when traveling west was a risky and dangerous ordeal.

Records indicate that Samuel S. Buckland settled on the site in 1859 and began ranching. He also established a tent hotel, which accommodated the wagon train settlers crossing the Immigrant Trail through Nevada, and a station for the Overland Stage Company.

During that time, he also constructed the first bridge across the Carson River that was downstream from Genoa.

By March, 1860, Buckland had erected a large ranch house that contained a trading post, tavern and hotel. He also agreed to allow the Pony Express to utilize his facility.

Additionally, on May 11, 1860, Buckland's Station assumed a minor, but important role in Nevada history. That day a group of men stayed overnight at Buckland's before heading to Pyramid Lake for combat with the Paiute tribe. The men requisitioned the Pony Express horses and headed north.

Four days later, the survivors of the skirmish, now called the first battle of the Pyramid Lake Indian War, straggled back to Buckland's. By summer of that year, the U.S. Government had decided to build a fort in Nevada to protect the growing population of the state from hostile tribes (who were only protecting their traditional homeland from the onslaught of settlers).

About a mile from the station, the U.S. Army erected Fort Churchill, which became the new stopping point for the Pony Express until the service went out of business in 1861.

In November, 1861, the Nevada territorial government designated Buckland's as the seat of Churchill County. This legal status stayed with the site until 1864, when Nevada became a state and true county lines were drawn (which placed Buckland's in Lyon County).

In 1870, Buckland built the present two-story structure, which was originally a hotel with dance hall, dining room and saloon. Interestingly, the hotel was constructed from wood sold at auction to Buckland for $750 by the U.S. Army when it decommissioned and dismantled nearby Fort Churchill.

The decline in stage traffic in the late 1870s marked the end of Buckland's Station as an important way stop. The building was later converted into a private residence and was inhabited until about the 1950s.

Today, the old station is partially boarded-up and suffering from years of neglect, but retains a certain charm. A worn wooden sidewalk/porch fronts the now-paved highway, still seeming to bid weary travelers to enter, relax, sit down by the fireplace.

The surrounding country remains agricultural; fields bordered by white fences and containing full, mature trees that provide shade and a sense of rural, farming ambience.

In the fall, groves of quaking aspen that line the nearby Carson River to the south turn a beautiful shade of yellow and give the entire area a warm, pleasant feeling.

Just across the highway is Fort Churchill State Historic Monument, where visitors can still find the adobe remains of the historic Civil War-era fort. A visitors center includes informative displays that show the original design and layout of the fort.

This park also contains a small cemetary, where Samuel Buckland and his family are buried.

For more information, contact Fort Churchill State Historic Monument, Silver Springs, NV 89429, (702) 577-2345. ❧

Soda Lake

The Rise and
Fall of
Soda Lake

SODA LAKE MAY NOT LOOK LIKE MUCH more than a
small desert lake, but its existence tells a lot about the history and
development of the Fallon area.

Not truly a natural body of water, Soda Lake was created by a
combination of factors, including the presence of natural springs,
the effects of mining its depths for soda — starting in the 1850s —
and a rising water table caused by irrigation of the area.

The lake's many unusual and historic features have also made
it the subject of discussions in recent years to make it a park and to
place it, and a submerged soda works factory, on the National
Register as a place of significant historical, scientific and recreational interest.

Soda Lake is located about 55 miles east of Carson City via
Highway 50 and Soda Lake Road, a marked paved street that is
five miles west of Fallon.

Originally part of a collapsed volcanic crater, the lake's

modern history begins in the middle of the last century. In the 1840s, settlers crossing the nearby 40 mile desert stumbled upon the lake as well as the natural springs adjacent to it — which were the first fresh waters to be found after crossing that dreaded stretch of desert.

In the mid-1850s, several claims were filed on the lake because of the presence of remarkably pure soda, which could be used in the mining operations on Virginia City's Comstock Lode.

Starting in 1875, commercial soda extraction operations commenced on the lake and two major soda works were constructed — making it one of the west's first commercially significant soda producing sites.

Records indicate that soda from the lake was of such quality that it won a gold medal at the 1876 Centennial exposition in Philadelphia.

Ironically, the completion of the Newlands Water Project in 1915, which helped spur the development of the surrounding Lahontan Valley as an agricultural and ranching oasis, marked the beginning of the end of Soda Lake's namesake business.

Irrigation water from the massive aqueduct system, which brought water to the desert valley from the Carson and Truckee rivers, percolated into the groundwater and caused the lake level to rise.

Within a few years, the soda factory was submerged, an occurrence that resulted in several landmark decisions, including the legal precedent that absolves the U.S. Government from damages as a result of "unintentional" actions.

In the end, the lake level rose from 147 feet to more than 200 feet, leaving the soda works under some 35 feet of water.

As a result of being under water, the soda works are well preserved. Over the years, the lake has become popular with divers who can swim through the relatively intact ruins of the old soda plant and other buildings.

Additionally, divers report the presence of a "ghost forest" at the southeastern end of the lake which is believed to be the remains of a grove of cottonwood trees.

Photos of the soda works and trees are on display at the nearby Churchill County Museum in Fallon and depict a mysterious, murky underwater world filled with strange shapes and shadows.

Because of its undeveloped nature — submerged soda factory notwithstanding — the lake has become a sanctuary for a wide variety of birds. During a recent visit, I spotted flocks of gulls, terns, ducks and other waterfowl enjoying the peace and calm of this half-hidden lake.

The lake also boasts a population of brine shrimp and underwater plants that have adapted to the high alkali content of the water.

For more information about Soda Lake, contact the Churchill County Chamber of Commerce, 100 Campus Way, Fallon, NV 89406, (702) 423-2544, or the Churchill County Museum, 1050 S. Maine St., Fallon, NV 89406, (702) 423-3677. ❧

Tallac Historic Site, Lake Tahoe

Tallac's
Magnificent Mansions

By THE TURN OF THIS CENTURY, America's rich had discovered the beauty of Lake Tahoe. Hundreds of magnificent vacation homes sprouted around the lake, including a handful of particularly impressive structures built on Tahoe's south shore.

These buildings, sitting in the cool shadows of Mount Tallac, eventually included the lake's first casino and hotel resort, an estate so fabulous that some jokingly called it the "Vatican Lodge" and a rustic, two-story lodge appropriately named after the home of the Norse Gods ("Valhalla").

Fortunately for us, many of these marvelous homes and buildings have been preserved as part of the Tallac Historic Site, managed by the U.S. Forest Service. The Tallac Historic Site is located off Highway 89, just north of Camp Richardson.

Strolling the historic grounds is an opportunity to step back in time to imagine an era before the automobile and the airplane, when only the very wealthy could afford to vacation in exotic and difficult to reach locales — such as Lake Tahoe.

There is a peacefulness and beauty to the area and, as you walk through the tall pines, listening to the lake waters lapping at the nearby beach, you can't help but ponder how it might have been to own a little piece of Lake Tahoe.

The Tallac story began in the 1870s, when a fellow named Yank Clement opened a hotel on the south shore, called the Tallac Point House, to accommodate visitors to the lake.

In addition to steamboat rides and a saloon, "Yank's" also boasted one of the finest dance floors in the area.

In 1880, however, "Yank's" was sold to Elias "Lucky" Baldwin, a California entrepreneur and avid gambler. Baldwin immediately began recasting the shaded lakeside inn into something much grander.

Within a few years, Baldwin had expanded the hotel into a 250-room resort that catered to the wealthy. By 1903, he had added a two-story casino that included a ballroom, four bowling alleys, sun parlors and billiard rooms.

About the same time, in 1894, George Tallant, son of one of the founders of Crocker Bank, built a rustic, but comfortable, summer home nearly adjacent to the Baldwin property.

In 1899, it was sold to Lloyd Tevis, who expanded and renovated the home, making it the largest and most luxurious in the area. He also added numerous outlying buildings, including servants quarters, a dairy, stables and a wonderful garden area with Japanese tea houses and arched bridges.

In 1923, the Tevis home was sold to George Pope Jr., a San Francisco lumber and shipping magnate. To reflect his rather ecumenical name, the estate was nicknamed the "Vatican Lodge."

Meanwhile, in 1923, another prominent businessman, Walter Heller, also arrived at Lake Tahoe and purchased the land south of the Pope estate. Heller began construction of what would become the last great Tallac mansion, a massive stone and wood lodge named "Valhalla."

The early 1920s not only marked the heydays of the magnificent Tallac homes, but also the end of the "Lucky" Baldwin era. In 1920, "Lucky" Baldwin's daughter, Anita, decided to close the resort, which had began declining, and had the buildings completely demolished.

Later that same year, Dextra Baldwin McGonagle, a Baldwin granddaughter, constructed a beautiful single-story home on the family property.

For the next four decades, all three of the estates were exclusive lakeside vacation homes for their respective owners. In the late 1960s and early 1970s, however, the large homes ceased to be economical for the families and gradually they were turned over to the U.S. Forest Service.

The end result is that today we can enjoy the beauty and quiet majesty of these picturesque estates. All three are classic examples of the early 20th century "Tahoe" architecture, which utilized native stone and wood to blend into the surroundings.

A paved bicycle path connects each estate and is highlighted by a series of excellent interpretive signs that tell the history of various sites and buildings.

The Baldwin-McGonagle home is now a museum, offering original furnishings, a small gift shop as well as changing art exhibits and an informative Washo tribe display (the area was originally the home of members of the native Washo tribe).

The latter includes a Washo Garden exhibit that shows various plants on which the tribe subsisted and samples of traditional housing (the "galis daigal" winter lodge, consisting of bark and pine poles, as well as the "gadu" summer home, made of sage and branches).

The Pope estate is the largest of the three areas and includes the greatest number of surviving buildings, although none are open to visitors at the present time. Volunteer efforts are ongoing to maintain and restore the historic structures.

Nearby "Valhalla" remains perhaps the most impressive of the three estates with its huge main hall and floor to ceiling stone fireplace. The main house continues to be used for community events, including concerts during the summer months.

The Tallac site also includes a number of picnic grounds and public beaches. For more information about the Tallac Historic Site, contact the U.S. Forest Service, P.O. Box 8465, South Lake Tahoe, CA 95705, (916) 544-6420. ❧

Fallen Leaf Lake

Fabulous
Fallen Leaf
Lake

TUCKED IN THE MOUNTAINS, a few miles from magnificent Lake Tahoe, is another body of water that just might be — with apologies to Mark Twain — the second best "fairest picture the whole earth affords."

Called Fallen Leaf Lake, this picturesque alpine lake rivals its larger neighbor in beauty. In fact, if not for a fluke of nature, namely a small stretch of land that separates Fallen Leaf from Tahoe, the area could easily have been another Emerald Bay.

Fallen Leaf Lake is located five miles west of Highway 89, immediately north of Camp Richardson on Lake Tahoe's southwest shore. A marked and paved road is located directly across the highway from the entrance to the U.S. Forest Service Visitors Center and Tallac Historic Site.

The U.S. Forest Service also operates a developed camping area at the northeast end of Fallen Leaf Lake. The entrance to the 206-unit campground, which is open from May to October, is located about a quarter-of-a-mile north of Fallen Leaf Lake Road, off Highway 89.

The drive from the highway to the lake is pleasant, passing through large pine trees. About three miles from the turn-off, you travel by a lovely aspen grove and open meadow, both of which are spectacular in the fall, when the aspen leaves have turned gold.

The road narrows as it reaches the east end of the lake and, after passing into a residential area, you catch your first glimpse of the lake. As you drive, you can see incredible scenery, including Cathedral Peak (the southern shoulder of Mount Tallac) rising over the lake, its 9,785-foot crown mirrored in the lake's crystal waters.

I think it is the "mirror effect" of Fallen Leaf Lake that makes the view so remarkable. Rather than enclosing the lake, the reflection of the surrounding mountains seems to stretch into infinity and create a sense of being in a much larger place.

While much of the lake is private property, you can continue to drive to the lake's west end where, in the summer months, Fallen Leaf Lodge offers accommodations and a marina. In the winter, the lodge is closed, but you can park and enjoy the marvelous views.

About a half-mile from the end of the road (it comes to a deadend at the Stanford Sierra Resort, a private retreat), you can turn west on another narrow (all the roads around here are extremely narrow, so be careful while driving) paved road, lined by large log railings.

This road leads to Lily Lake, a trailhead for hiking into the nearby Desolation Wilderness and, most surprising of all, an elegant waterfall (which, according to E.B. Scott's excellent, "Saga of Lake Tahoe," is called Modjeska Falls after a famous Polish actress of the late 19th century).

Frankly, even if Fallen Leaf Lake didn't exist, the waterfall would be worth a visit. Located just north of the road on Glen

Alpine Creek, which feeds into Fallen Leaf Lake, the joyous, rolling waves of falling water are an impressive and unexpected sight.

While the falls aren't as large as Horsetail Falls (which are located at the south end of the Desolation Wilderness, visible from Highway 50, near Twin Bridges), they are, nonetheless, unique and beautiful.

You can park off the road here and hike to the waterfall. From the top, the view of the rapidly cascading water as it falls down the lush canyon is worth noting. Across the creek, you can also see private homes — people fortunate enough to be able to look out on the waterfall any time they want.

The road continues west, paralleling Glen Alpine Creek, for another mile or so to Lily Lake. Opposite the creek, parallel to the road, is a jumbled mountainside of loose boulders and stones, wonderful for casual rock climbing (I know my four-year-old son loved it).

A concrete bridge marks the end of the road. On the north side of the bridge, you can park and hike a short distance to Lily Lake, a small, but quite photogenic lake literally cupped in the mountains.

The main Glen Alpine Trail leads northwest from here, north of Lily Lake, into the Desolation Wilderness. While we didn't continue from here, maps indicate a second waterfall, about a half-mile farther, and Glen Alpine Springs, a mineral spring and former sheep camp, located about a mile west.

For information about camping at Fallen Leaf Campground, contact the National Forest Service, (916) 544-5994. For information about Fallen Leaf Lodge (which operates a private campground with 37 sites, open June through late September), call (916) 541-3366. ❧

Virginia and Truckee Railroad,
Virginia City

"Queen of the Shortlines" Keeps on Puffing

BOB GRAY DESERVES A LOT OF CREDIT for stamina. Since 1972, Gray and his crew have been gradually rebuilding the historic Virginia & Truckee Railroad line down the hill from Virginia City — making it the only shortline railroad in the country that is still growing.

His goal is to eventually run his steam train from the old V & T freight depot on Sutton and E Streets (just down the hill from Virginia City's main commercial district on C Street) to Mound House on Highway 50 and, eventually, into Carson City.

A non-profit group is working with Gray and various local government officials to acquire the property rights and secure the financial commitments that would allow the train to run from Virginia City to Carson City.

The railroad recently took a major step closer to making Gray's dream a reality with the completion of the line into Gold Hill. The train now runs from a small depot on F Street, just south of

255

the St. Mary's in the Mountains Catholic Church, to the Gold Hill Depot (a half-hour ride that covers about 10 miles).

The task hasn't been easy. More than a year ago, the V & T line had extended a few miles down the hill and reached the entrance to the original Tunnel 3. Gray and his workers began reconstructing the tunnel, hoping to reopen it last summer.

But the tunnel, which has a history of trouble, refused to cooperate and Gray found it was safer and more prudent to extend the track around the hill, avoiding the tunnel.

The result is an even more spectacular trip as the train slowly sweeps around the side of a hill, offering a panoramic view of Gold Hill and the surrounding environs.

From there, the train continues across Highway 342 — a railroad crossing also had to be constructed for the extension — and stops at the original Gold Hill Depot, which has been restored into small shops and businesses.

Additionally, Gray hopes next year to push the railroad line a little farther down the hill to a large open-pit mine below the depot, then construct a turn-around for the train.

Of course, none of this would be particularly notable except for the fact that there's something unique and appealing about a vintage steam train. The chugging of the engine, the sound of the whistle and the loud sigh as it relaxes after a hard run are all reminders of an earlier, simpler time.

Today's Virginia & Truckee line is pulled by Number 29, an oil-burning steam locomotive that was built in 1916 by the famed Baldwin Locomotive Works in Philadelphia (in fact, the first 16 engines used by the original V & T Railroad were Baldwin locomotives — the best of that era).

While Number 29 was never used on the original V & T line, the engine has performed well for the past several years (the line started carrying passengers in 1976), hauling a two-car load (an open car or an enclosed caboose) ten times each day during the summer months that the line operates.

Travelers are also treated to an informative talk during the ride as the conductor relates anecdotes about the Comstock and points out places of historic interest along the way, including original mining headframes, mill sites and other buildings.

Records indicate the original V & T Railroad began carrying freight, gold and silver ore and passengers in 1869. The railroad was built to service the fabulously rich Comstock mines, taking ore to distant refineries and mills.

The V & T's route eventually stretched from Virginia City, through the winding Carson River corridor, to Carson City and north to Reno. Later, a spur connected the line to Minden and Gardnerville.

By the 1870s and 1880s, the V & T became known as the richest railroad in the world because of the enormous mineral wealth it carried out of Virginia City (it was also known as the "crookedest" railroad in the world, not because its owners were corrupt, but because of all the twists and turns it took in traveling down the hill from Virginia City and through the Carson River corridor).

By 1938, however, Virginia City had ceased to produce a sufficient quantity or quality of ore and the line was discontinued from Virginia City, with the tracks removed the following year. In 1950, the V & T made its last run from Carson City to Reno and the remainder of the tracks were removed.

The Virginia and Truckee Railroad operates daily from May through the end of September. The first train departs at 10:30 a.m., with the last departing at 5:45 p.m. Cost is $3.50 for adults, $1.75 for children and $7.00 for an all-day pass. For information, call (702) 847-0380. ❧

Nevada Books

Give the Gift
of Nevada

BOOKS MAKE GREAT GIFTS and there are many good ones dealing with Nevada that you may want to consider for those hard-to-buy-for Nevadaphile friends and family members.

The pool of available Nevada-related books encompasses a wide variety of topics ranging from historical novels to travel books to poetry to western fiction.

The following is not any kind of comprehensive listing of every book about the Silver State (although there is such a publication, "The Nevada Bibliography," prepared by Stanley W. Paher and available from Nevada Publications). Rather, this is my somewhat eclectic listing of books I've found to be either interesting historic material for the hardcore Nevada reader or just fun reading.

First on the list would have to the previously-mentioned Stanley Paher's "Nevada Ghost Towns & Mining Camps." This is the definitive book about exploring the state, filled with great photos, history and anecdotes about hundreds of mining towns that once dotted the Nevada landscape.

The book has been in print for more than two decades, but remains largely accurate in its descriptions of the remains of Nevada's ghost towns (although disregard his highway designations, which are outdated).

Paher also has written a fun historic book about Las Vegas, called, "Las Vegas — Where It Began." This volume is filled with solid historic information and a wonderful collection of vintage photographs of the sleepy little spring that became Las Vegas.

Another good historical resource is "Virginia City and the Silver Region of the Comstock Lode," by Douglas McDonald. Also published by Paher's Nevada Publications Company, the book provides a good overview of the rich and colorful history of Virginia City.

McDonald's book contains a wealth of historic photos and drawings that tell about the discovery of silver in the shadow of Sun Mountain and the development of the town that was once the richest and most exciting in the west.

Equally interesting is "This Was Nevada," by Phillip Earl. Written by the Curator of Exhibits of the Nevada Historical Society, this book is a collection of more than forty of Earl's weekly columns about Nevada's history.

Within its pages, readers will learn how Tonopah was named, the story of Nevada's last lynching and why Delamar was a lousy place to work. The book also contains 45 historic photos and drawings.

A more narrowly focused historic book is "Nevada Newspaper Days," by Jake Highton. This 323 page book tells about the early days of newspapering in Nevada and continues up to the present (with some rather candid observations about the current state of newspapers in Nevada).

The last historic book on my list is the Nevada Historical Marker Guidebook, published by Falcon Hill Press of Sparks. This thin booklet answers the question that all seasoned travelers through Nevada have asked — what the heck was written on that historical marker before it was shot up with bullets, sandblasted by the winds and faded by the sun?

For those who enjoy driving, hiking and walking across Nevada, there are several quality travel books about Nevada. A personal favorite is David Toll's self-published, "Compleat Nevada Traveler," a humorous and informative book about the small towns and historic sites in the state. This book is periodically updated by the author.

Another book I can recommend is "Touring Nevada," by Mary Ellen and Al Glass. While less personal than Toll's, this book provides useful directions and information about scenic and historic places found throughout the state.

Of more recent vintage is Deke Castleman's second edition of "The Nevada Handbook," published recently by Moon Publications. This is a handy (no pun intended) guide to the state which includes information about everything from hotels to restaurants to camping to historic sites to shopping.

Castleman has also written "Las Vegas," a guidebook for the Compass American Guide series. The book combines standard guidebook information (hotel listings, show descriptions) with a wickedly candid, revisionist view of the history and development of the city.

Of a more technical nature are "Hiking the Great Basin," by John Hart for Sierra Club Books and "The Tahoe Sierra," by Jeffrey P. Schaffer for Wilderness Press. Both books are excellent sources for specific hiking information on Nevada.

There are also a handful of fiction books which clearly capture the flavor of Nevada. Perhaps the first, and still one of the best, is Mark Twain's "Roughing It."

Written more than a century ago, "Roughing It," remains funny, witty and remarkably contemporary in its views about Nevada. It is also probably the most quoted-from book ever written about Nevada.

Of a more serious nature is Walter Van Tilburg Clark's "Oxbow Incident." This western tale about mob justice vividly incorporates the dramatic Nevada terrain. Clark, who lived in Nevada for most of his life, clearly understands the qualities that make the state more than just a place.

No collection of Nevada books would be complete without the works of Robert Laxalt. A former newspaper reporter and magazine writer, Laxalt is considered the state's best living author and has a string of acclaimed novels, including, "Sweet Promised

Land," "A Cup of Tea in Pamplona," "A Man in the Wheatfield," "In a Hundred Graves: A Basque Portrait" and "Nevada: A Bicentennial History."

His most recent work, "Basque Hotel," is a heartfelt portrait of Carson City (Laxalt's hometown) in the 1930s. With a colorful cast of characters and a richly-painted setting, it may be his best book (until his next one).

Equally literate is "Desert Wood," a collection of the works of Nevada poets, published by the University of Nevada Press. While the poems aren't always about Nevada, the book provides a sampling of some of the excellent material being produced by the state's finest and most creative poets. Yes, there is culture in Nevada.

My last recommendations are perhaps my quirkiest. In recent years, Nevada has become known as the home and birthplace of the Cowboy Poetry Gathering in Elko.

While this uniquely western folkart can be an acquired taste for some, there are two volumes of traditional and contemporary cowboy poetry that I have enjoyed because of their sincere, folksy honesty.

The first is "Cowboy Poetry: A Gathering," by Hal Cannon, founder of the Elko event. This book contains dozens of poems about life on the range and ranch, and was developed from poetry readings during the first Cowboy Poetry Gathering, held in 1985.

The second is "Waddie Mitchell's Christmas Poems," a slim booklet written by Nevada's most well known cowboy poet. While only 57 pages long, the poems offer an authentic slice of cowboy life and philosophy. Both cowboy poetry books are published by Peregrine Smith Books of Utah.

All of these books are available or can be ordered at local bookstores or through the catalogs of the University of Nevada Press, Nevada Magazine and Nevada Publications. ❧

About the Author

RICHARD MORENO is the author of *The Backyard Traveler Returns* and *The Backyard Traveler: 54 Outings in Northern Nevada*, and is currently at work on *The Backyard Traveler Ghost Town Companion*, a collection of photos and stories about Nevada ghost towns, to be published in late 1993. He is also working on an as yet untitled book, with photographer Larry Prosor, for the University of Nevada Press. He is the publisher of Nevada Magazine and previously was director of advertising and public relations for the Nevada Commission on Tourism and an award-winning reporter for the Reno Gazette-Journal.

He resides in Carson City with his son, Hank.

The
Backyard
Traveler
Returns

*62 outings in Southern, Eastern
and Historical Nevada*